ANE COMPACT OF VILLANY

ANE COMPACT OF VILLANY:

THE HISTORY OF ARGYLL'S OUTLAWED GANG

LINDSAY CAMPBELL

Copyright © 2015 Lindsay Campbell

The moral right of the author has been asserted.

Apart from any fair dealing for the purposes of research or private study, or criticism or review, as permitted under the Copyright, Designs and Patents Act 1988, this publication may only be reproduced, stored or transmitted, in any form or by any means, with the prior permission in writing of the publishers, or in the case of reprographic reproduction in accordance with the terms of licences issued by the Copyright Licensing Agency. Enquiries concerning reproduction outside those terms should be sent to the publishers.

Matador
9 Priory Business Park,
Wistow Road, Kibworth Beauchamp,
Leicestershire. LE8 0RX
Tel: 0116 279 2299
Email: books@troubador.co.uk
Web: www.troubador.co.uk/matador
Twitter: @matadorbooks

ISBN 978 1784624 279

British Library Cataloguing in Publication Data.
A catalogue record for this book is available from the British Library.

Printed and bound in the UK by TJ International, Padstow, Cornwall
Typeset in 12pt Bembo by Troubador Publishing Ltd, Leicester, UK

Matador is an imprint of Troubador Publishing Ltd

MIX
Paper from responsible sources
FSC® C013056

Grateful thanks are due to the following people whose input to the research and writing of this work has been invaluable:

The staff of Oban Library, past and present.

The staff of Argyll & Bute County Archives, past and present.

Mr. Tony Dalton, Maolachy.

The owner-occupiers (as they were in 2000) of the gang's targets.

The staff of Inveraray Jail Museum.

Mr. Jeremy Thompson and the staff at Matador.

And most of all my mother, whose interest in the doings of 'Lachie and the boys' has been unfailing.

ONE

The damp green hills of the district of Lorn in Argyll have hidden many secrets over the centuries. In the closing decades of the 17th century, they hid a gang of over a dozen desperate outlawed men. But these were no honourable Robin Hoods fighting the authorities for social and political justice. They were thieves in the worst sense – callous, greedy, blackmailing "stouthrieves" to use the old Scots term, outcast from society and literally draining the livelihood from their own already beleaguered countrymen and women. Their reign of terror covered some of the most politically and economically unstable years in the history of the West Highlands, and despite the impact on the rural communities, the authorities and society in general, the memory of the gang's activities has been largely forgotten. Justifiably, one might say, but the history surrounding the gang, the society they moved in, and the men, the authorities and the system which eventually overcame them tells a story which epitomises West Highland life at the time.

One can hardly begin any study of Scottish history, especially the history of the salt-battered, rain-drenched county of Argyll, without failing to mention the powerful Clan Campbell. In this county bordering the west coast and hemmed in by Inverness-shire, Dumbartonshire and Perthshire, it was Campbells in their many forms who owned a good deal of the land and Campbells who held the high posts in government, law and the Church. One could hardly step ashore or cross a river without stepping on someone's Campbell territory. It was indeed Campbells who turned the wheels of Argyll society, whether their enemies liked it or not.

By the last quarter of the 17th century, the Campbells had feuded with every other large and powerful clan in the county and beyond, for they were certainly not the only landowners in Argyll. By nature, the nobles who led and served the clan were vindictive but wily in battle, loyal and with good business acumen at home, and with forward thinking minds and silver tongues in the debating chamber or at court. Their religious affiliation was largely to the Presbyterian Church, and so successful had their business dealings been that for many decades, whenever a Campbell noble or gentryman lost his seat of power, neighbouring clans would take every opportunity to fill the vacuum.[1]

Doing so of course, made the neighbouring noble or gentryman an enemy of the Campbells and to make an enemy of a Campbell was to settle one's destiny for decades. The feuding between Campbells, Lamonts, MacDougalls, MacLeans and MacDonalds in the 17th century was bitter and violent, with atrocities on all sides equal to any told by legend and folklore, many of the feuds bolstered by the age-old cause of religion. Some hundred or more years after the Reformation had hit Scotland, the two main protagonists, the Presbyterians and the Episcopalians, had political adherents prepared to take such issues to the top level of government. When these political allies reached the top level, one religious denomination would wreak terrible and bloody persecution on the other, only for counter persecution to occur when the tables were turned.

Another cause for minor warfare in the glens at the time were the clashes between the old Highland clan system which was merging (uncomfortably at times) with the Norman-style feudal system, both being slowly and enforcedly adapted to the pressures of a modernising society. The basics of both the clan and the feudal system were similar of course, and in many ways it was only in practise that they differed. At the top of the tree in both cases was the king, or at least the Crown, from whom the nobility held their lands and titles. These latter honours were inherited, and the Head of the Family would retain a portion of the land for his own necessities and rent out the remainder to the gentry who also held these high ranking tenancies by heritage.[2]

The gentry in their turn retained part of the land and buildings for their own necessities, some actually getting their hands dirty at the plough or in the byre, and using the profits from it to pay the rent back to the nobility, among other purposes. The property of the lairds could vary from a single farmtown to several scattered over the parish, and in this case the 'tack' or land and associated buildings, was rented out in turn to 'tacksmen' (tenants).[3]

In his turn, the tacksman, who may sometimes be quite well off if his tack was a good one, would farm the area, earning his own income and paying his rent to the laird from any surplus. If there were enough dwellings in the tack and the land needed several farm-workers, the tacksman might well sub-let a cottage or two to the lowest level of farmer, the humble cottar, who usually only had enough money to pay the rent and feed himself and his family from his wages and the wee scrap of land infront of the 'cott'.

The basics of a system such as this were far from unique to Scotland or even the UK, and when the climate was favourable, the economy bouyant, the political situation calm and everyone got along well with everyone else, it worked brilliantly.

The clan system similarly worked well if all aspects were good. The clan chief was at the head, whilst below him, the gentry (the lairds) were usually descended from his younger sons. Not unlike the feudal system, a chief's younger sons would often be farmed out to other gentry, brought up in a semi-working class environment and treated as cherished foster sons. The bonds thus made would reinforce family ties and business deals and made for a complex, chivalric respect for one's enemies, backed by a culture of kinship stronger than that in the feudal system.[4]

The tacksmen and cottars below the lairds were usually related to each other, if only distantly and because of the intermarriage that naturally takes place in any rural community. Such rural communities as those surrounding the Highland chiefs meant that the gentry at least would be on first name terms with their tacksmen, and the tacksmen would know their lairds and chiefs by their nickname, the latter being more widely used, even across the biggest social divide. So firm was the loyalty of many clansmen for their chief that they'd follow him readily to battle, protect his person from invading usurpers and trust in his reciprocal support in time of need [5]. Nevertheless, one hasn't heard a put-down line until one's heard it from an auld Highland wifie to her high-born laird who's perceived to be getting too big for his boots!

In practise of course, neither the feudal system nor the clan system worked perfectly all the time. All it took was the king and the nobility at the top or the gentry and low-born folk at the bottom to interfere with the smooth running of life and the whole system would be overturned. If a noble came into the displeasure of the king, his land would be taken off him and given to another, usually a sworn enemy, meaning the new chief would be in charge of his enemy's vassals. Often he'd evict them and put his own people into the tacks, dispossessing a whole community in one fell swoop and creating more enemies for himself. If the economy or the climate meant that the lowest born cottars couldn't pay their rents, the tacksmen above them couldn't pay theirs in turn, nor could the gentry afford to pay the nobility.[6]

As such therefore, both the clan system and the feudal system survived on delicate footings, the clan system also tying in with the equally delicately balanced tradition of retributive thieving in the West Highlands. Much has been written about this proclivity for clan theft which the Highlanders and West coasters had, and in the 17th century the lawlessness of this part of the country was legendary and spoken of half in derision, half in fear by city folk. Similar to the clan and feudal systems working well when all parties and economic and climatic surroundings were conducive, the retributive theft idea was well and good in theory, and if taken in small measure worked brilliantly. The practicalities of terrain and communication (if not travel) in Argyll meant that it was usually quicker, cheaper and often more merciful to handle criminal complaints locally. At the very least, a 17th century tacksman pursuing a case for the theft of a goat or the odd cheese via the proper process of law would involve more time, effort, and money than it was worth, possibly leaving a penniless, distressed family to be supported by the community at the end of it all. How much simpler, quicker and more merciful all round was it for the targetted tacksman to go over the hill one afternoon a few weeks later and steal a couple of chickens in return for his missing goat. A few extra hours work for the retributive thief, fewer eggs for the target family for a while and honour was satisfied. If further action was taken, it was usually just a matter of the local gentry going in search of the stolen goods on behalf of the offended tacksman, and either leading the thieved animal home or getting some sort of recompense for it if it was already in the cooking pot.[7]

Of course, even this simple retributive thieving was exploited from time to time by people who clearly knew how to work the system. One common trick was to offer 'tascal money'. A secret friend of the thief's would pretend to find the stolen animal or at least know where it was, present it or the information to the owner and when a reward of thanks was offered, accept it graciously – only to return half of the money to the thief[8]! No doubt local gossip would prevent any efforts the 'finder' of the animal made from withholding more of the reward than he was entitled to!

The Argyll justiciary records of the 1670s are filled with this kind of petty thieving and local retributive justice; there appears to be more salmon poaching and brawling at this time than the serious crime of later decades and the punishments are certainly far more lenient – a couple of horses stolen from a neighbour may only pull in a hefty fine, whereas twenty years later, the thief would be hanged with barely any finesse of witness or jury.

Undoubtedly the cause for the rise of West Highland lawlessness in the late 17th century was the clan warfare and politics which had wreaked so much violence and havoc on the district. To uphold the clan honour, retributive theft was taken to its furthest extent. Not simply a case of a tacksman stealing his neighbour's goat, entire clans would range over the hills of a neighbouring clan, burning, demolishing and ruining land and dwellings, killing, kidnapping and ousting people of all ages, genders and abilities from their cottages, and returning home with as much cattle as they could drive, and as many valuables as they could carry – only to be subject to a counter attack themselves the following summer.

Apart from the vast clan raids which were of course concentrated within the county itself, in time, some clans became notorious for taking their raids out of the county. By the 1670s, a key part of the rural economy was becoming too much of a temptation to such clan raiders. For as long as the dairy and beef industry has existed in the Highlands, Islands and Argyll, the practise of 'driving' the cattle to market, however far or near that market may be, has been a vital part of the farming year. Although the cattle were driven almost year round for better grazing or the small local markets, it was the September gatherings in Perthshire which drew the largest crowds of men and animals. The drovers, their lads and the accompanying dogs and ponies would often be local to the area from where the cattle came, sometimes even the gentry themselves (or professional drovers in later years), and their passage through the countryside on the way to the great markets has engendered many a legend and specialist study. As a team, the drovers and their cattle would cover around ten miles a day, herding anything from a few dozen to several hundred head of stock along ancient hill routes, staying at well recognised change-houses or droving inns, whilst their four-legged charges massed in the fields around, then leaving the county by one of a few routes. Half the time, the innkeeper's silver spoons or his daughter's honour also left with the drovers, but recompense was guaranteed, since the men had to stay at the same inn on the way back![9]

With such quantities of valuable stock as the drovers were herding out of the county, it didn't take the warring clans long to realise that here was another source to be thieved – and not just the valuable stock belonging to one's enemy clan.

Before long, those clan raiders who'd swarmed over the hills to despoil an entire glen, were swarming out of the county by the same route the drovers used, to hijack their cattle on the way to or from market. The wiser clans waited until someone had bought the cattle at the market and were then driving them home to an adjoining county, before they ambushed them and drove the same stock to their own home-grounds instead.

The raiders were usually well organised, sometimes funded by a member of the local gentry as their patron, and with a notorious thief or 'cataran' as one of the ring-leaders; some clans became so adept at this large-scale cattle rustling (the MacEans of Glencoe and the Camerons were notorious for it) that the issue was taken to government level[10]. The catarans were beginning to penetrate into Lowland districts, and to begin with the clan chiefs turned a blind eye to it all; the whole country was suffering due to the clan and Covenanting Wars, and because of the economy if nothing else, suddenly finding yourself with several hundred head of extra cattle on your land was hardly a disadvantage. The concerns of the nobles were at first towards national politics, and whether they would be sitting in their own castle with their head on their shoulders next month, not what their clansmen were doing at market, but when more clans began to jump on the cataran's bandwagon, and more vicious thieves started to become involved in what was increasingly a serious threat to the stability of the whole region, then the clan chiefs had no choice but to sit up and take notice. The victims of large-scale cattle-thieving it was claimed 'compounded with the thieves' [11] at first, probably following the age-old practise of thief-bote in which the victims of crime agree not to report the incident, so long as the goods are returned to them unharmed[12]. By the 1670s however, even the most hard-nosed of these victims was beginning to press the nobles for some sort of protection.

Efforts had already been made to impose some degree of lawfulness on the Argyll and Highland hills – an Act of Parliament had been passed, attemptedly making the parishoners of areas where the thefts occurred and those through which the thieves passed with their booty, responsible for pursuit of the rustlers, on pain of making good the loss to the victims. The latter were supposed to sue the gentry and the gentry recover the value of the goods from the thieves when they were caught. Such laws made few dents in the Argyll justiciary system and the massive cattle thieving continued apace. The MacEans were raiding as far as Aberdeenshire, and one noble started blaming another, both at court and at home. Eventually, the Privy Council in Edinburgh authorised the son of the recently executed Marquess of Argyll to raise sixty men for the protection of the county, an effective standing army, to respond with as much heavy-handedness as they wished to the cattle thieves. The main exits and entrances into the county were to be 'watched' by bands of recruited soldiers, bolstered by local gentry and all were very properly organised and trained; commissions were issued, lieutenants appointed and arrangements made to pay the men's wages. If these Watch-keepers were informed within 36 hours of any theft, then, like with the previous Act, they must regain the stolen goods or repay the value of them from the forfeited possessions of the convicted thieves.[13]

Those entrances and exits in and out of the county where the Watch-keepers were stationed were probably part of the same ancient drove routes which had also borne ordinary foot traffic for centuries, such was the convenience of the old roads. In the very North, bordering Inverness-shire, the drove (and undoubtedly cattle raiding) route went via Glencoe and Rannoch Moor, its desolate surroundings even today being somewhat daunting. Another route went through the Pass of Brander and Dalmally, leaving the county at Clifton or Tyndrum. A third route picked up several smaller branches leading from Ford, Glenfeochan or the land West of Loch Awe, all meeting at Inveraray to leave the county at Tarbert on Loch Lomondside, passing over Hell's Glen or the Rest and Be Thankful en route[14]. In addition to these Watch stations (probably therefore at Tyndrum, Tarbert and Rannoch Moor) there would probably have been a few smaller exits out of the county eg. at Inverinan, Glen Fyne or the many small sea routes around Dunoon.

With the county guarded and served by trained bands of regular soldiery or willing tenants and gentry, the Watch-keepers, their officers and commanders were so successful at first that in 1668, the government in Edinburgh declared Argyll and the surrounding counties 'free from depradations'. If only! Within a year, someone found that "last year the thieves were only quiet because they were employed to keep the rest from stealing and for that had great liberties allowed them"[15]. In addition, many thefts went unreported, again probably due to thief-bote. Clearly however there was more to it than simple ingrained lawlessness on the part of the Argyll folk – the invading Earl of Atholl, it was rumoured, was actually organising massive cattle raids, and there was talk of blackmail, while the current Duke of Argyll wanted Atholl's job on the Justiciary Board. In the end, Sir James Campbell of Lawers got the choice position, and with the help of the Duke of Argyll began to have some qualified successes. Thieves began to be caught, officers commissions were renewed, wages were raised, more Acts of Parliament passed to support the security measures and in the middle of the domestic quarrels which fostered the Highland Wars of the 1670s, the Watch-keepers slowly and carefully solidified their hold on the country passes through the hills which had been the scene of so much violence and clan raiding.[16]

The thieving was far from ended, but by the close of the 1670s, politics rather than cattle thieving was more in the foremind of the county's nobility. The civil war which had been raging, inspired by various causes but all indirectly coming down to religious denomination, local politics and clan warfare, had seen some nobles lose their heads on the block, others at the head of armies on a battlefield, others brought to bankruptcy or accused of out and out treason. The upshot for a county such as Argyll was that martial law was imposed to overcome the clan raiding, the violence of the civil war turning friend against friend and leaving the low-born tacksmen and cottars to bear the brunt, financially. And yet there was more to come: with the supremacy of the Episcopalian cause at court, the Presbyterians were now the persecuted ones and before long, the persecution of the 'Covenanters' (those Presbyterians who'd signed the National Covenant, a parliamentarian document which stated that there should be no interference by the king in the affairs of the Presbyterian Church of Scotland) reached its zenith. The Covenanting Wars had already bespoiled vast tracts of countryside, but now, small communities which wouldn't have otherwise seen warfare, witnessed their ministers burnt at the stake for the faith, and congregations slaughtered. In the Lowlands of Scotland, the Duke of Monmouth was defeating Covenanting armies, royal militia were being raised across the country, and after domestic quarrels with the MacLeans over the latters' debts, the Duke of Argyll and the Duke of York (the future King James II) fell out over religion.[17]

The Scottish Privy Council in Edinburgh introduced an Act, which should have satisfied all, but not the Duke of Argyll. After his argument with the Duke of York (an open Roman Catholic), he insisted that royalty should not be exempt from the Oath of Allegiance to the Crown; the Oath contained an anti-Popery clause. Argyll's enemies took this move as a sign of treason and applied for a commission against him, forcing him to sign the Oath himself, which he did several times, arguing and arguing against the claims of treason, but with his enemies succeeding in tripping him up every time. Eventually, he became a wanted man and subsequently escaped to London and thence to Holland, leaving his duchy to the bloodthirsty politics of the time.[18]

By 1683, the Duke of Argyll was still in Holland and had been raising support. He wasn't the most consistent of military leaders, but he had enough power to make the Privy Council believe he was going to invade and a militia was raised against him, headed in Argyll by the same Earl of Atholl who'd almost caused the collapse of the Watch-keeping security and to whom certain tenantries in Inveraray had been given. Once in the town however, Atholl began throwing his weight around, gathering up all Argyll's former supporters and letting them know who was now boss. Various Campbell gentry were arrested, the countryside around was scorched and devastated and tales are told of tenants' wives and children evicted without even the clothes they stood up in, cattle stolen or killed on the spot, and crops and buildings razed[19]. As a county, and with the height of the Covenanting Wars being rightly dubbed The Killing Times, Argyll was rapidly turning into a battlefield, so that the successes of the Watch-keepers against the clan cattle rustlers were failing again. There was even an attempt to introduce such a strict control on the movement of any cattle, that the entire economy of the county would have ground to a halt, and the 'foreign' occupiers of tenantries and castles wouldn't be receiving any rents. Appeals were therefore made to allow certain men to move beasts to and from market (including some Campbell gentry in Nether Lorn) and some were even allowed to stop others if they didn't have a pass to move the beasts.[20]

From out of this volatile and unstable background comes a gang of raiders and freebooters who by April 1690 are well known in Lorn and Argyll as housebreakers and thieves[21]. Ring leader of the gang is Lachlan 'Cuttach' Campbell (the Gaelic nickname 'Cuttach' could indicate that Lachlan was either left-handed or simply had the evil personality, so often (erroneously) associated in the old days with anything and anyone 'leftie'). With him on this occasion came John Campbell, 'Dugald Campbell in Lorn' the latter clearly a tacksman, and both of whom may have been relatives of Lachlan's, Donald MacNokaird and John MacLauchlane. For reasons unspecified by documentary sources and unclear otherwise, these notorious stouthrieves somehow met up with Duncan Clerk, a tacksman in Stronsaul and his son John, possibly at one of the many local markets and fairs.

The little farmstead of Stronsaul is now a suitably remote pair of cottages on the Dunoon peninsula, tucked beside a rough unmetalled track and thick in a forestry plantation. A rumbling burn goes by and smoke creeps out of its chimney as it must have done when Lachlan's gang turned up at the Clerk's door in spring 1690.

Duncan and his son had already done a few local raids of their own in the district. Just three years earlier, the pair made their way one night over the hill to the neighbouring farmtown of Ardnadam (not exactly where the current Ardnadam stands but near enough) and took at least a barrel of dry corn and probably some mutton and goat flesh. Had it not been for the corn, this may have been taken by the authorities as a simple retributive theft, but a barrel of grain would be quite a valuable item, worth several months wages to a farmworker[22], and clearly Duncan and his son had the wherewithal to own or borrow a pony to carry it back to Stronsaul. Not quite the sort of thing one could turn a blind eye to. Nor was their next raid: poor Donald Lamont, a fellow tacksman in the neighbouring farmtown of Lecknagall, was woken up one night by raiders with blackened faces. Amid warnings to the farmer and his family to keep quiet, Duncan and young John got clean away with half a barrel of beef, two stone of butter, one and a half plaids, some money and three pieces of cloth[23]. The plaids alone would have paid Donald's own income for the quarter year, and left the family without a much needed extra blanket in the winter's cold, while the money may have been the rent due to his landlord.

Quite why the Clerks weren't arrested after the Lecknagall raid isn't stated in the records. Obviously someone came calling at Stronsaul after the Ardnadam theft and found the meat and corn rather naively stashed away there, probably in Duncan's byre, but whether the Lamont's were too frightened to report 'their' raid, or whether they simply accepted it as a retributive one, isn't clear.

Despite Duncan's naivety at hiding the Ardnadam loot in his own byre, one wonders if Lachlan Cuttach Campbell, having met the Clerks, saw the promise of a skilled thief in young John; Cuttach and Duncan MacNokaird certainly took John on a raid to Lochstreynshead one night, soon after coming to Stronsaul.[24]

Lochstreynshead was the site of much conflict and local politics in the 17th century, being a change house at what is now the head of Loch Striven on the same Cowal peninsula; many a Campbell gentleman with his forces had passed by in the warring decades prior to Cuttach's raid. Although it seems an unlikely spot for such an attack (the hills either side are too gentle and there doesn't appear to be an easy overland escape route, or ambush site), as a change house, there would have been goods, plenishings and money aplenty for the face-blackened thieves breaking in by night to tie up the changemaster Alexander Campbell and his wife and servants, then range the property over for anything saleable or gainable. Money, cloths (including some small linens – naive Duncan Clerk still insisted on keeping some at home!) and other items were taken back to Stronsaul.[25]

Young John's namesake, another tacksman in Dunloskinbeg was also targetted around this time, losing five pecks of pease, some nets and a goat to the same three men who broke into the Streysnhead change house.[26]

Over the course of the next year or so, John Clerk died; it's never specified how or under what circumstances, but during the same year it appears that Cuttach and his gang left Stronsaul to the ineptness of Duncan Clerk, who eventually found himself on trial at Inveraray. There, he confessed all his crimes in the presence of baillie Colin Campbell of Ellangreig, and a jury of eleven Inveraray men, two Campbeltown men and two others. Many of the jury would stand again in future trials, and are recorded as part of Inveraray life at the time (the merchants John and Robert Brown, and the former provost William Brown or a Duncanson merchant; some of them are buried locally).[27]

Duncan Clerk's admission of guilt brought an inevitable result; he was hanged on the afternoon of 4 July 1691.[28]

With John Clerk already in his grave and his father swinging on the Inveraray gallows, the people who suffered at the Clerks' hands and the authorities which convicted them may have thought, despite the growing notoriety of Cuttach's people, that the worst was over. How wrong could they have been.

FOOTNOTES

1. HCC, p. 38.
2. Ibid. pp. 162-167.
3. Ibid. p. 94.
4. Ibid. pp. 166-169.
5. For example, the legends recorded in "Records of Argyll" by Lord Archibald Campbell, published by Blackwood and Sons, Edinburgh 1885, pp. 16-18, 33 or 42.

6. Glencoe and EHW, pp. 13-14.
7. Hearkening back to a far older (and ironically, feudal) system of justice, this local system was taken to extremes at times, when alleged murderers or traitors were dealt with clan chiefs, not always in the most merciful manner. See Glencoe and EHW, p. 17.
8. Glencoe and EHW, p. 13 and "A Dictionary of the Scottish Language" by John Jamieson, edited by John Johnstone, published by William Tait, Edinburgh 1846 p. 537 (accessed via Google books).
9. Drove Roads e.g. pp. 35-38.
10. Glencoe and EHW, pp. 42 and 29.
11. Ibid. p. 31.
12. "A Dictionary of the Scottish Language" by John Jamieson, edited by John Johnstone, published by William Tait, Edinburgh 1846, p. 554 (accessed via Google books and listed under "Thiftbute").
13. Glencoe and EHW, pp. 31-33.
14. Drove Roads, pp. 87-92.
15. Glencoe and EHW, p. 49.
16. Ibid. pp. 49-51.
17. Various sources e.g. HCC, p. 27.
18. Collins Encyclopaedia of Scotland edited by John Keay and Julia Keay, published by Harper and Collins, 2000, p. 134.
19. HCC, p. 60.
20. Ibid. p. 39.
21. Just Rec, p. 137.
22. www.johnhearfield.com/History/Breadt/htm
23. Just Rec, p. 137.
24. Ibid. p. 137.
25. Ibid. p. 137.
26. Ibid. p. 137.
27. The Royal Commission on the Ancient and Historical Monuments of Scotland volume 7, Mid Argyll and Cowal, medieval and later monuments published 1992, pp. 117-118, entry no.65.
28. Just Rec, p.138.

TWO

The windy, suntrap of a place which is modern Inveraray sits on a headland South of the castle, the river Aray and the wooded slopes of Duniquaich on one side and Loch Fyne bounding the very streets of the town on another, whilst roads lead out to Lochgilphead, Oban and Perthshire. This fine, black and white-painted town throngs with visitors every summer, and is still subject to the same 'prodigious' rainfall and 'variable' [1] climate it was in former centuries, and probably also on the day when Duncan Clerk was hanged.

Inveraray as we see it now, however, is (unsurprisingly) a world away from the Inveraray of the closing years of the 17th century. Made into a royal borough in 1648, the town has long been the product of its landowners, local and national history and, more tellingly, its position as the legal centre of the county. Although the fishing industry was the day to day income of the town until relatively recently, Inveraray's place as a legal centre and hub of cultural niceties further boosted the economy. Most significantly of all though to the criminals of Argyll, was the position of the town at the mouth of the Aray. Modern Inveraray is not only a world away from 17th century Inveraray, but several hundred yards down the road as well; the town was quite literally carted away by the Duke's demolition teams in the 18th century, leaving only a few river-drowned foundations, re-used stones and the local burial ground adjoining the site of the original church.[2]

Inveraray Castle, similarly, is a re-build on a new site, not too far from the old. The 15th century castle which once sat within the bounds of the original town was, by the end of the 17th century a battered structure with a high tower in typical Scottish tower-house style. The years worth of ill-treatment by successive warring occupants can hardly have helped the somewhat precarious nature of the castle masonry, and at the end of the 17th century the state of the castle was no doubt as dire as it was in the earlier years of the 18th when the Duke's architects despaired of repairing the enormous rents and crumbling stonework.[3]

Tucked next to the castle the town of Inveraray at the time was centred around the medieval mercat cross, in itself surrounded by a triangular market place, with rows of thatched fishermen's cottages, artisans' dwellings and small-time taverns dotted down the street towards the loch with smarter stone-built properties closer to the castle and the public buildings. These latter comprised two churches (one for the English congregation, one for the local Gaelic speakers), as replacements for the old medieval church, with at least one of them adjoining the castle yard with a tower and its own burial ground. The tolbooth, built after 1648, appears to have been just to the south of the churches and similarly adjoined the market square at the highest point of the old town. This building was a low structure of two stories with a crow-stepped gable and an external stair and housed the justiciary court (complete with 'fenced' dock for the accused [4]), a gaol and probably a room or two for adminstrative purposes, though it seems that these may have been in short supply; even the jury were wont to retire to one of the churches next door at the end of a hearing. Over the years, these three buildings in the old town appear to have represented the important twin powers of church and local justiciary.[5]

As respectable a town as 17th century Inverarary sounds on paper, it was woefully unable to keep its smart image intact. There were no bridges over the river[6] which would have slowed communications considerably and probably brought the place to an economic standstill occasionally. The people lived a hand-to-mouth existence and poverty was widespread, many of the tenants living in cottages little better than hovels. Despite the efforts of the Church authorities, education was at rock-bottom and even in the early years of the 18th century, there were only ten men in the whole parish who spoke English [7]. If a crisis occured in climate, economy or local politics, the expectation that the town would repair its own streets, public buildings and harbour from its own revenue could not be kept – like so many other small rural towns of that era, there simply wasn't any revenue to do the repairing with.

The legal system which Inveraray was the heart of, had been through some troubling times by the end of the 17th century. Although the town was the site of a twice yearly baronial court and the Duke or Earl was its hereditary head, the travelling court which had tried criminals so successfully before the time of King Charles I had lapsed somewhat after his execution and there were certainly no such visits to this west circuit by 1690. There were, however, twice weekly sheriff courts (the Duke was also the hereditary sheriff), and when the political situation allowed and the Earl of Atholl wasn't beating seven bells out of any Campbells who came his way, various other semi-legal gatherings found their way to Inveraray, many of the city men appalled by the poverty and state of the buildings in the town.[8.]

In practise, the courts which sat in the tolbooth at Inveraray, or at least sat when the town wasn't occupied by enemy beseigers, was usually headed by a deputy of the Duke, professionally trained or otherwise [9]. Criminals which the authorities judged worth hunting down could be declared outlaw and fugitive in their absence, with their names fixed to the stone-built mercat cross (presumably on a paper glued to the stonework, or on a permanent nail fixed in the masonry; it probably got blown into the loch many a time!), a horn was sounded three times and an announcement made with three loud proclamations of "Oh Yes" [10.]; one wonders if it was done in Gaelic and English! If the criminal was brought to court it was often by his gentry landlord or one or two of his more law-abiding neighbours or via the success of the semi-military Watch-keepers policing the exits and entrances of the county. The accused would be housed in the gaol at the tolbooth or in the castle dungeon or any other convenient place, often in appalling conditions, and if he didn't manage to escape would be brought to court under guard and stood in the 'fenced' dock for his trial.[11.]

In the seat of justice, heading the court at the end of the 17th century, was often Mr John Campbell of Moy, a noble in his own right, and a man of much legal experience, having been in the job since 1674 [12]. Occasionally in the closing years of the century when national politics were calmer and Inveraray was occupied by Campbells again, the Earl of Argyll himself sat over the court with his brother John Campbell of Mamore; another noble (including Campbell of Ardkinglas) might take on the task temporarily if they and the usual deputy justiciar were absent.[13.]

The fifteen men of the jury who sat in the tolbooth court were taken from the town or its immediate vicinity, unless the accused was from considerably outwith the district. Often the jurors were the same well-respected merchants, tenants and artisans, doing their jury service time and again. Infact their repeated use not only makes one wonder what work they managed to get done in their ordinary life if they were forever being called up for jury service, but perhaps such repeated service was as a result of them being the few who could speak both Gaelic and English easily enough to fully understand the proceedings.

When all evidence had been dealt with and whatever was going to be recorded had been (statements weren't always noted down fully, and confessions were usually made verbally to a high-ranking official), the jury returned their verdict and the accused was brought back into court. Even for relatively serious crimes the verdict wasn't always a foregone conclusion, though in the years soon after The Killing Times and during famine and economic depravation, the speed and ruthlessness of the sentences do sometimes seem harsh to the modern mind. In many other Scottish courts it would be Mr.Hangman, in his role as 'dempster' (clerk of the court), who would proclaim the sentence from the sealed paper he'd been given, to the trembling figure of the accused. This, however, doesn't seem to have been the case at Inveraray, and it was the actual clerk of court who read the verdict [14]. If capital punishment was decided on, then the accused would be returned to the gaol overnight, before making his or her final journey (not always at dawn or dusk) the following day via the classic wooden cart with made-ready coffin, to the gallows. It seems as though the family of the executed criminal would afterwards be given opportunity to remove the corpse for private burial [15], although all his moveable possessions were confiscated in order to help redress the expense of the hearing, and to go towards compensation for the victims. If a proclamation of outlaw had been given, it's doubtful whether the criminal would be allowed any contact with his friends or family, even after death, and his remains would probably rot away until the next sorry figure came trundling along in a coffin-laden cart from the tolbooth.

This nicely organised legal system which operated at Inveraray in the closing years of the 17th century had been somewhat disorganised barely half a generation before. Certainly the years in which Lachlan Cuttach Campbell and his gang of stoutrieves had been living with Duncan Clerk at Stronsaul had seen some of the most violent and significant events in the Highland Wars of the 1670s and '80s. The Highland supporters of the Roman Catholic James II and the Argyll or Lowland supporters of the Presbyterian King William and Queen Mary had clashed both at court and on the battlefield several times; nobles had been exiled or lost their heads, clans had been warring against clans, enemy parties had invaded and been beaten back and scandalous rumours had scorched round the country about King James' queen and their newly born heir, causing a rumpus in wider politics. By the end of 1689, King William of Orange and Queen Mary were on the throne in London, whilst the supporters of the now-exiled James began the struggle which led them to bear the name Jacobite.

Despite the accession of a 'foreign' king and the instability of local politics, everyday life was rather calmer all round at the beginning of the 1690s, at least in Argyll and at least for the law-abiding citizens of the county, so that the justiciary records are kept more regularly, and the rising criminal activity coming from the unstable political situation of a few years before could be controlled more efficiently, despite the extra efforts of those self-same criminals. The increasing effectiveness of the Watch-keeping patrols is clear when someone, somewhere was able to apprehend the ring-leader of a certain gang of stouthrieves. One Lachlan Cuttach Campbell was imprisoned in the castle at Inveraray in spring or summer 1693 [16]. Not for long; he escaped, probably with the help of his gang members, and probably also assisted by the doubtful nature of the castle masonry. Undeterred, he was hunted down and caught again a year or half a year later, this time imprisoned in the town gaol by authorities probably aware of his escape method last time. The more secure surroundings of the tolbooth however didn't foil Cuttach or his gang; he was on the loose again before he could be brought to trial.[17]

Before and shortly after these episodes of imprisonment, quite what Cuttach's gang were up to in the district isn't clear. Later records indicate that he may have already started a protection racket, retrieving unpaid dues in kind by stealing the possessions of his debtors [18]. Local tradition also points at either his gang, or a similar one, operating locally around this time in the hills above Glenfeochan. A shieling was raided of its dairy products (almost certainly before c.1697 [19]), the thieves fleeing along a peat track bordering the glen, and accidentally dropping part of their haul. It tumbled down the hillside and landed in a gentle, green patch by the river soon dubbed The Dale of the Cheese by locals ('Dal-na-cabaig') [20]. Other stories tell of a vicious gang of thieves who made their headquarters in the ruins of a castle on an island in Loch na String high in the hills between Loch Avich and Loch Scammadale [21]. With the site's proximity to all Cuttach's soon-to-be-recorded stamping grounds, and the story being that the Loch na String gang ranged over the whole county and even into adjoining ones (which they may just have done, though there's little documentary evidence for it), it seems highly likely that the castle on the lochan above Loch Avich was the centre of Cuttach's nefarious world.

This same Loch na String which may have been Cuttach's headquarters is one of the larger hill lochans in Lorn, currently sitting among forestry trees and beside the hill route popular with walkers known as The String of Lorn. The low-lying island at its centre, around 150 yards long and shaded with mist even on the aerial photo on Google Earth, displays 'no visible signs' of masonry, while the 'time-worn ruin' there in 1845 was probably plundered to the ground for local works a few decades later. Access to the island (discounting a boat) was probably along a sunken causeway on the east, but there may recently have been another hidden causeway at the south-west, judging from a tiny spot of a second island marked on the Pathfinder 1991 map [22]. The 'castle' on the main island which Cuttach and his gang may have occupied (probably originally just a small tower-house) was unlikely to have been built by them, and by their time may have been simply the two storey remains of an accompanying dwelling on the site. In Lorn, if a traditional stone-built property loses its roof in the gales and isn't subsequently repaired, the walls can be quickly eroded by further wind and rain damage. Within fifty years, a roofless, two storey structure can be down to the top of its first storey, and within a hundred or so years, the walls of such a ruin can be reduced to around three or four feet high. Quite how tall the walls of the 'time worn ruin' on the island were in 1845 isn't stated in the source, but it seems entirely viable that a building last used in Cuttach's day, would still be visible, if much ruinous, by the mid 19th century. Yet again, the irony of history plays a part in Cuttach's choice of headquarters, and indicates that he may have been a local boy before embarking on his criminal career. The route of the String of Lorn was the site of a pitched Campbell battle in medieval days, a conflict so bloody that it entered local legend. One of the Campbell chiefs was killed and the location of a small island 'castle' not far from the battle-site perhaps indicates that the original structure was there (whether before or after the battle) for minor defensive purposes. Being so easily defended, and on a frequented trade route, but well away from population centres or sea-access, if Loch na String was indeed Cuttach's headquarters, he couldn't have chosen a better spot. [23]

Although the bloodthirsty decades of The Killing Times and the strife of the Highland Wars undoubtedly spawned many criminal gangs, the question remains where exactly did Cuttach originate from? Whether or not his was the gang which occupied the castle on Loch na String, undoubtedly he did the bulk of his work in Nether Lorn, and certainly his earliest recorded, and later most active, work seems to have been based on the rolling, wooded green hills between Loch Feochan, Loch Fyne and Loch Melfort. He, or someone important in the gang, clearly knew the hill routes (the smaller ones threading through tiny scrubby glens as well as the main thoroughfares used by the drovers and merchants); he knew the small local markets and ferry ports, which farmtowns and shielings were barely used and even whose land and cattle was whose. Although there were a fair number of criminals haunting the Argyll roads, brought in from outwith the county when e.g. the Earl of Atholl's men predated the district a few years previously, Cuttach does appear to have been a local man. Quite how local no-one will ever know, but two curious facts exist which point out his possible origin.

Over the hill from Loch na String the farm of Bragleen Mhor and its satellite Bragleen Beg were in the 17th century the base of the gentry family of Campbell of Bragleen. The head of the family at the time, Colin Campbell, was a close compatriot and supporter of the Duke of Argyll. He and his brother had business dealings with other gentry in the district at the time, being mentioned in several bonds and legal papers [24], and his family had married into the MacDougalls of Corrielorn on the shores of Loch Arkaig. In the early 1690s, as part of the Duke of Argyll's work suppressing the early Jacobites on the orders of the Privy Council, Colin Campbell of Bragleen was sent to occupy a MacLean castle on Mull [25]. He and his clansmen were there for many months, and with Bragleen being so close to Loch na String, who knows what blackmailing deal may have been struck between his tacksmen at home and Cuttach's men while he was away. Something was clearly going on at Bragleen around this time, since the farm and its tacks stand out in the gang's ten year recorded history as never being targetted once. Certainly, the strange situation of a wealthy gentryman's farmstead right in the middle of the gang's home ground apparently not being touched by them indicates that either Cuttach was enacting a fierce (and always obeyed) extortion racket from them, or that he had some other close connection with Bragleen.

The 17th century saw the initial rise of the infamous highwayman culture in Britain, immortalised by later, almost legendary figures, well known to Hollywood and tourist information centres. Many of the major towns and cities were predated on their outskirts by such thieves on horseback who didn't stop at murder to achieve their ill gotten gains and the typical highwayman of the 17th century was far from being the dashing 'gentleman of the road' of legend. He was often a dispossessed, or at least displaced, son of the gentry, deprived of his true heritage by being on the wrong side after some skirmish, or simply gambling away the family assets, committing a crime or two, then taking to the hills. He would classically have enough military experience to enable him to command a few assistants, know how to handle a gun and ride like the wind; he would also be educated enough to know what to do with the money and saleable goods in order to prevent him and his gang coming up against the authorities at the first instance [26]. It may therefore be that Cuttach, with his clear skill at organising and commanding a group of his fellow stouthrieves, was one of these sons of the gentry, dispossessed by any number of conflicts and quarrels over the past decade in Argyll. Though there was certainly no loyalty in him for his fellow clansmen, and he targetted gentry and tacksman and poor travelling merchant alike, it may be that the reason Campbell of Bragleen's farmstead, so close to the gang's headquarters, was spared any recorded or legendary raid by the gang, was because he had family there.

Whatever Cuttach's family origin, he would have needed to be trained in his iniquitous skills by some other experienced stouthrief, and just as he was stated in the justiciary records in later years to be a "nurserer of many thieves", so another such "nurserer" was active locally just a few years before Cuttach comes to the attention of the courts. One Archibald Macnicol in Kenmore was living on Mull as a notorious thief with his gang in 1680 and predating farmsteads there and on the mainland (Inveraray and Kilbride are mentioned – perhaps the Kilbride near what is now Oban). Archie was stated to have entertained and kept correspondence with "thieves, vagabonds and broken men, receiving and harbouring them within his dwelling house". Quantities of men, (strangers to the district) were seen frequenting his house at the dead of night, "and concealed by him [from his law-abiding neighbours]". One can't help wondering, if Archie's men strayed onto the mainland as the documentary sources state they did, whether Cuttach learnt his trade at that same cottage in Kenmore at the "dead tyme of night".[27]

It was also around this time that a man who similarly appears to have been local, although perhaps further North in the district than Cuttach himself, joins the gang. Hugh Cameron, a seemingly young man, is first recorded as being part of the gang in early summer 1696 [28]. One of his name is recorded as being part of an independent raid a few years before, but that Hugh Cameron, the son of a brewer at Dunstaffnage, was caught and hanged before Cuttach's compatriot joined the gang. It wasn't unknown for a supposedly hanged criminal at Inveraray to come back to life [29], but one would imagine that if this had been the case with Hugh Cameron from Dunstaffnage, someone would have mentioned it in the justiciary records! Hugh may however have been a relation to his afore mentioned namesake, since at the time he's first recorded as being part of the gang, they conduct a raid on a property only a few miles away.[30]

One night in May or June 1696, an empty house sitting on the banks of the River Awe at Polfearn, was broken into. The house was owned by the Earl of Breadalbane and stored there was "a considerable quantity of salmon". Needless to say, there wasn't a considerable quantity of salmon after Cuttach and his gang had left!

This raid raises a number of questions. Firstly, since nothing else was taken (not even the odd fishing net or rope) it was probably a targetted raid, with someone in the gang having fore-knowledge about the place and what it contained. Two of the gang members who came with Cuttach and Hugh on the night of the raid were from Appin, or it may be that Hugh was indeed related to the Dunstaffnage brewer's son and had local, North Lorn, knowledge. Polfearn wasn't the gang's usual stamping ground, indicating that, whether the Appin men or Hugh had been the lynchpin on this occasion or not, the man with the foreknowledge may well have been in the vicinity recently, listening and watching the ordinary people of the parish. Were gang members constantly on the look-out for profitable information, infiltrating local communities at market or in the inns? As the propaganda posters said in WWII: "Walls have ears"!

Just a few weeks later, the same two Appin men (John and Archibald MacColl) who'd been with Cuttach, Hugh and the others, went on a raid at the opposite end of the gang's stamping ground. The vast Moor of Leckan stretched (and still stretches) high in the hills between Loch Awe and Loch Fyne. At the time, it was the site of one of the larger, but local, drove routes which took travellers across the desolate, wet and windy bogs and open land onward to the south approaches of Inveraray. Criss-crossed until very recently by smaller hill tracks connecting the shielings and remote dwellings where travellers could gain shelter if they were be-nighted en-route, the moor had long been a dangerous place for the law-abiding people of Lorn. Grazing there in June or July 1696 were a few horses belonging to Alexander Campbell of Sonachan or his tenants on land which was actually Sonachan land [31]. Campbell of Sonachan was a gentryman with an old family descended from Campbell of Cawdor and whose seat was down on the shores of Loch Awe. Alexander and his family had been staunch supporters of the House of Argyll over the decades, one of them had been in charge of the Watch-keeping regiments in 1682 (attemptedly preventing such activity as Cuttach's gang were enacting) [32], he'd been part of the anti-Jacobite insurrection of the Earl of Argyll in 1685, and got fined heavily for his pains by the then-Jacobite government after Argyll had been executed [33]. In later years, he was one of the signatories on an Oath of Loyalty to King George at the time of the First Jacobite Rebellion [34]. In short, Campbell of Sonachan was a Royalist whom one didn't quarrel with readily.

Despite this, there were three less Sonachan horses on the Moor of Leckan after Cuttach's men had been there one day, and with three men conducting the raid, it's easy to imagine how they got to their next target, on the far side of Inveraray. The curiosity (or perhaps the sheer chutzpah!) of the situation is that to get there, the three gang members would probably have had to pass through the town of Inveraray, riding past the gallows on the loch-shore and a few yards from the very tolbooth itself. As for their next target, the farmstead of Maam (still sitting in Glen Shira on the shores of Loch Fyne and still a working business) was also Sonachan land, tenanted by a Campbell vassal. The tenant however, one Dugald MacKellar, was far from an angel himself. One of his neighbour's daughters had been flirting with him one day, an argument had ensued (fortunately it seems Dugald wasn't yet married!), the girl had been struck, her father and brother had intervened, there were drawn dirks, a sword and Dugald had been de-bonnetted, but otherwise no-one was hurt. In court, the men got fined £12, the girl £6 and all ordered to behave themselves in future [35]. Perhaps Dugald was trying too hard to behave himself and hadn't paid Cuttach the protection money, for the gang stole a mare from the farm.

The other gang member who'd conducted the Sonachan raids with the Appin men was John Ban MacIntyre the farrier, otherwise known as 'Good Sollar', a half Gaelic nickname translating as 'Good Provider'; John certainly became an experienced gang member, going out with Cuttach on the later raids, armed to the teeth and living up to his 'providing' reputation. The irony of his monicker, however, may have been lost on the men who, a day or two later, tracked the gang down to the shieling of Inishalongairt, ten or twelve miles away on the hillside above Glenfyne, and almost at the county boundary [36]. Cuttach himself may well have been with them at the shieling (if he was, it explains why he didn't do the raid himself, since the gang would be passing through Inveraray where he'd recently been in custody) since he was back behind bars by October the same year. Cuttach being who he was of course, he wasn't behind bars for long – the court weren't even sure, when the records were written up in later years, in which prison he was kept (or perhaps no-one wanted to admit the insecurity of their dungeon!).

All these raids which Cuttach's gang were conducting over the hills of Lorn, whilst certainly not the naive raids of the Clerks, nor the retributive thefts so common among otherwise law-abiding tacksmen of Argyll, were hardly the huge, bloodthirsty strikes of their later years. The plenishings and property they stole were a vital part of the livelihood of the tacksmen and their families, and Cuttach's crimes could hardly be said to be victimless, but rural working people the world over are used to repeated hardship, and the fact that very few of the early raids were reported points to the locals resignedly accepting such a way of life. The political climate in and around Argyll was slowly stabilising, the Highland Wars of the previous decade were being fought now in the court rooms or in Edinburgh, and a Campbell was nominally sitting in the castle at Inveraray again. Emerging from all this stability however, Cuttach's gang would soon make even the gentry look over their shoulders and fasten the door-bolts more securely at night. Lachlan Cuttach Campbell, not the Campbell Watch-keepers, would soon be ruling the Argyll hills.

FOOTNOTES

1. "The Second Statistical Account" volume 7, Renfrew-Argyll, published by Blackwood and Sons, Edinburgh 1845.
2. "The Royal Commission on the Ancient and Historical Monuments of Scotland" volume 7, Mid Argyll and Cowal, medieval and later monuments, 1992.
3. "Inveraray and the Dukes of Argyll" by Ian G. Lindsay and Mary Cosh, published Edinburgh University Press, 1973, pp. 25-26
4. Several references in Just Rec, eg. p. 185.
5. "Inveraray and the Dukes of Argyll" by Ian G. Lindsay and Mary Cosh, published Edinburgh University Press, 1973, pp. 20-21.
6. Ibid. p. 23.
7. Ibid. p. 23.
8. Ibid. pp. 23 and 21-22.

9. Just Rec, pp. XII-XIII.
10. Just Rec, p. 184.
11. Several references in Just Rec, e.g. pp. 157 or 192.
12. Just Rec, p. 41.
13. Several references in Just Rec, e.g. p.131.
14. Just Rec, p. XIX.
15. A legend exists in and around Loch Fyne that a certain Archie MacPhunn was hanged at Inveraray in the 17th or early 18th century, and during the process of his wife transporting his body back across the loch for private burial, he revived and went on to live many more years. Ref. website lamontcentral.activeboard.com/mobile.spark ('Half Hung Archie').
16. Just Rec, p. 162.
17. Ibid. p. 162.
18. Ibid. p. 186 ff.
19. Probably due to the famine at the time, this shieling (grid ref. 1923 7231) and others in the immediate vicinity would appear to have been abandoned and was certainly not noted on maps of c. 1750. Only its track from the south east remained by the time of the 19th century Ordnance Survey maps, and the site was rediscovered by the author in the late 20th century.
20. One of the inhabitants of Dalnacabeag (the late Kathie MacColl) recounted this story to the author c. 1985, and pointed out the peat track, visible at the time and crossing the hill on the opposite side of the glen.
21. "The Second Statistical Account" volume 7, Renfrew-Argyll, published by Blackwood and Sons, Edinburgh 1845, p. 64. The idea of the 'castle's' inhabitants being there 'nearly two centuries' has been referred to locally as 'two centuries' which may hint at the truth; Cuttach's gang would have spent time there both in the 17th and 18th centuries. The 'predatory incursions into adjoining counties' may refer to raids in Appin or at the far end of Glen Shira, or if another gang followed on from Cuttach's (e.g. the ones caught on Leckan Muir a few years later), the two may have become confused in oral history into the one.
22. OS Pathfinder 355 (NM 81/91 Kilmelford).

23. "Records of Argyll" by Lord Archibald Campbell, published by Blackwood and Sons, Edinburgh, 1885, pp. 172-173.
24. "The Clan Campbell Abstracts" by Sir Duncan Campbell of Barcaldine and Glenure. Accessible on www.archive.org?stream/clancampbellabst01camp_djvu.txt
25. HCC, p. 94.
26. "Underworld London" by Catherine Arnold, published by Simon and Schuster, London, 1997, pp. 81-83.
27. Just Rec, p. 114.
28. Ibid. p. 173.
29. See above, note 15.
30. Just Rec, p. 163.
31. Ibid. p. 162.
32. HCC, p. 34.
33. Ibid. p. 56.
34. Ibid. p. 106.
35. Just Rec, p. 141.
36. Ibid. p. 162.

THREE

As the final decade of the 17th century drew to a close, the political climate in Scotland was settling; but the real climate, the one of meteorology, was far from settled.

Always subject to varying weather conditions, with south westerly gales, mini-tornados and such heavy rainfall that hillsides regularly slide down onto roads, the West Highlands have never been best placed for perfect weather. Despite this, certain glens in summer were recognised in previous centuries as producing vast quantities of soft fruit and wonderfully plump cattle [1], and the Highlanders of old, with their ready access to fish and shellfish as a fall-back diet when the land wouldn't produce enough food, could usually ride out a short famine.[2]

In 1695 however, the harvest was a bad one. The people, high-born and low, would survive on the produce of the rivers and the lochs for a few months, but with no oats to barter and buy with, the economy would slow almost to a standstill, and ruination would threaten many a noble who relied solely on domestic revenue. Hopes would have risen for a better summer in 1696; it never came. That autumn, with precious little grass for the cattle to graze on, the income from the cattle-sales would be dire. Further bad harvests followed. By early 1697, Irish oats were being imported for the soldiers garrisoned up at Fort William, and the deaths from sheer starvation were beginning. The harvest of '97 was non-existent. The newly introduced potato crop rotted in the ground under the heavy snows and frost, the starving tenants didn't have the money to buy what food could be imported, and there were transport difficulties because of the weather. The gentry did what they could for their tenants, at least one of them forgiving arrears of rent and distributing what stock and crops he had and which would have otherwise been sold out of the county. Everyone was in the same boat and with no money coming in off the land, no cottager, tacksman or wealthy gentryman could pay his rent, no wages were paid out from it, bankruptcy was widespread and significant parts of communities were malnourished, if not already dead. By 1698, there was suffering all round and more to come; some areas are said to have been completely depopulated. Modern estimates indicate that anything from quarter to two thirds of the population died from starvation [3], and in one parish, the figures point to between 39% and 52% of farmsteads abandoned [4]. On Midmuir, one of the great passes through the hills commonly used by Cuttach's gang to rob travellers and drovers alike, only one of the two original farmsteads was still standing by the mid 18th century [5]. A corn kiln, seemingly abandoned in the middle of a bog close by, stands as silent testimony to the deprivation and utter misery of the famine years in 17th century Argyll.

Due to all this famine, and as with any period in

history when such natural devastation occurs, the crime rate rocketed. Clan raids, small-time retributive thefts and organised crime such as Cuttach's all increased; the empty properties, shielings and farmtowns were there to take refuge in with stolen goods, and the criminals didn't stop at theft. Murder and attempted murder was becoming common. Murder or no, the question that raises itself at this point is a practical one. In a time of such severe climatic disturbance as happened in the late 17th century, Cuttach's gang were able to travel vast distances, pounce on victims and disappear without trace into the hills, sometimes with considerable weight and quantity of goods. One can't help wondering: how on earth did they manage it? Communities were tight, everyone knew everyone else and everyone else's business. They knew the hills like we know our own high streets. Cuttach's gang must have had considerable influence on the locals and indeed their protection racket is acknowledged by the justiciary courts in their later trials. [6]

Undoubtedly the main technique for the gang, enabling this easy passage through the county, hearkens back to their time with the Clerks on the Dunoon peninsula. Several raids are reported to have been conducted 'under cloud of night', sometimes waiting in the vicinity of a target site until after sunset, sometimes just appearing out of the darkness, probably with the same blackened faces they had when working with the Clerks.

There are however several raids which appear to have been conducted in daytime, whether retaliatory ones against protection racket debtors or not. This begs the question: how did they manage to approach a farmstead in broad daylight without being seen? The answer is disturbingly simple, but one which modern day housebreakers thankfully appear to have forgotten about. Anyone who knows the Argyll hills well, will be familiar with the mist that moves at times like a living creature over the woods and down the crags, sometimes dispersing within seconds. When one is standing outside the mist, it appears thick enough to hide a whole farmstead, let alone a gang of stouthrieves descending from a crag. When inside it however, the mist itself is invisible, allowing easy movement by anyone who wishes to descend the crag and come onto the farmstead below without being seen. Anyone thus descending from the hills can be over the glen and into the mist on the other side within ten minutes, probably less if they were on a fast pony. A copycat thief, almost contemporary with Cuttach, is said in his original trial to have been 'favoured with rain and mist' on his final raid [7], whilst on early autumn mornings, one raiders' site not documented in the trials still has mist hanging low behind it and along the path the raiders descended from.[8]

In addition to both these principles (night-time raids and mist-hidden ambushes) it appears that the gang also used a technique which has certainly been forgotten by modern thieves, and infact probably hasn't been used by anyone for well over two hundred years. Almost all Cuttach's target sites have lowish but craggy upland areas close above and behind, with a track leading down from the high moors and another opposite leading up into another patch of moorland. Tracing their movements immediately before and after a raid indicates that the gang descended suddenly in a body from such a craggy upland area, sometimes wielding weapons at short range, did their work, then left via the opposite side of the glen, to meet up with their fellows or pick up a familiar track in the hills leading to a hide-out or back to their HQ.

Curiously, the technique used by the clans in battle (the infamous Highland Charge, which had its last flourishing at the likes of the battles of Killiecrankie or Keppoch) involved clansmen, led from the front by their gentry, storming down from an elevated position at short range, shooting pistols if they had them and wielding their swords when at close quarters. With such short range shock tactics, the Highland charge rarely failed, but if it did, they would return to the elevated position, or another close by. [9]

The apparent technique of Cuttach's gang (descending swiftly through the mist from an elevated position, wielding whatever weaponry they had, only to flee via another elevated position) sounds familiar enough to make one speculate whether Cuttach, Good Sollar or another longstanding gang member had some experience of a classic Highland charge.

Up until late 1696, whatever raids the gang did weren't reported as being particularly violent; perhaps they were violent, but their victims simply accepted it as part of the wider violence in society at the time. In November or December of that year however, John 'Good Sollar' MacIntyre and one of the Appin MacColls met John Campbell, a drover from Lismore whilst they were all at an alehouse on the mainland side of the ferry route to and from Lismore and Appin. Clearly John MacColl knew the spot (perhaps it was his 'local'), and they may well have been just as drunk as the drover, who at that time of year probably didn't have any cattle with him. He clearly had a purse on his belt though with a fair bit of money in it, which Good Sollar and MacColl relieved him of, in the process of beating him up. Drovers being the hardworking, hard fighting men they were, he doubtless fought back, but still lost his money.[10]

In the middle of all these raids, stouthrieving and blackmailing, violent or otherwise, arises the question of whether there was some other cause behind Cuttach's work. Although apparently no supporter of the mythical 'loyalty-among-thieves' principle, and certainly no political idealist, his targets when listed on paper, bear some striking similarities. The change house at Lochstreynshead which he raided with the Clerks in his early years, was on Campbell land, so was the farmtown of Dunloskinbeg and the estate of Ederlines from where he stole a single horse in 1690 or '96. The Moor of Leckan was Campbell land, as was the farmstead of Maam and the shieling of Inishalongairt where the Leckan and Maam horses were found. Down through the list of Cuttach's target sites, every place is Campbell owned or Campbell tenanted, sometimes both. Even the ones which don't appear to be, are owned by or tenanted by, family relations or vassals of Campbells. One is even tenanted by a MacGregor who'd changed his name to Campbell, hinting at the political machinations associated with rebellious MacGregors and the fact that many more law-abiding MacGregors changed their names to Campbell, to avoid their landlords being forced to evict them in line with a Privy Council ruling [11]. This latter issue had been part of the Privy Council's backlash against the Earl of Breadalbane's propositions in his clan reconciliation plots, and it hints even further at Cuttach's initial motive for his criminal career. Almost every one of the Campbell targets which his gang attacked were anti-Jacobite. Tellingly, he avoids Kintyre altogether – a Jacobite stronghold at the best of times – and the one exception to the anti-Jacobite raids he conducts is the Polfearn salmon raid. On that occasion, the haul was taken from Breadalbane property, and at that date, the Earl of Breadalbane (that formerly staunch Jacobite) had just been exposed as the double-dealing betrayer of the Jacobite cause that he was – the clans were turning against him, and all the faith the early Jacobites had in his representation at court, had been shattered. Was this Polfearn salmon raid Cuttach's own private retaliation against Breadalbane's wheeler-dealing?

Sir John Campbell of Glenorchy, the infamous Earl of Breadalbane to his fellows, was a mature man by the time the Highland Wars of the 1670s were raging. From early in his career he'd been distrusted both at home and at court; even his own father said he was intelligent and talented, but dishonest [12]. His quarrels at court almost brought him to ruin and after threats of treason, he climbed back up the social ladder again with great difficulty and with the hated Earl of Atholl as an ally. Throughout the 1670s and '80s whenever there were bonds, bribes and domestic intrigue flying around, John Breadalbane was always at the centre, wheeler-dealing to the best of his ability, as an out-and-out Jacobite. The hope of the Jacobites however died at the Battle of Killiecrankie, understandably disquieting their noble supporters all over the country. In the middle of all the anti-Jacobite fervour, Breadalbane returned home, declaring himself ill with gout, and anyway he was neutral. No-one believed him, especially when he was involved in another rising, resulting in another rout on the battlefield for the Jacobites. Breadalbane fled home again with an arrest warrant on his head, after a futile attempt at pacifying King William.[13]

Still this didn't prevent his double-dealing. For quite some time, John Breadalbane had been playing his own game in the Highlands, pretending that he was thick in a project which would mollify the clans and set up a truce between them and the Royalists. He'd been negotiating with various clan chiefs and Privy Council members, but eventually when holes began to appear in all his wheeler-dealing, his reputation with both the clans and the Privy Council took another dive. The dramatic crumbling of Breadalbane's clan reconciliation plan only proved to the Jacobites themselves that his efforts on their behalf were empty promises and part of a big anti-clan plot [14]. This time, the finger-pointing worked, and Breadalbane had another accusation of treason levelled against him. Within months, he was behind bars in Edinburgh, talking his way out of a trip to the block. He was still talking a few months later, but by then (1697), the clans and nobles back home in Argyll were beginning to solve their differences and get on with the day-to-day difficulties of life. Bail for Breadalbane began to be discussed and the day came when he could leave his prison [15]. The dangerous and colourful character which was John Breadalbane, wasn't seen meddling and double-dealing at court again. Perhaps, after what had happened to his colleague and distant relation a few years before, he thought himself lucky to escape Edinburgh with his head still on his shoulders.

With the Earl of Breadalbane suitably taught a lesson, the Jacobite Cuttach and his men continued targetting the more classic Campbell or anti-Jacobite properties in Argyll. One could argue that with the business success of the Campbells, there was so much of their land in the county that any stouthrieves raid would come up on Campbell property. Indeed, one only has to look at a list of other place names at the time (eg.from the Minutes of the Synod of Argyll) to see that an average of 78% of properties in mainland Argyll would be Campbell owned. Over 99 % of Cuttach's target sites were anti-Jacobite Campbell associated; the only remaining ones, history doesn't relate the political leanings of their landlords. [16]

The figures speak for themselves, and although it doesn't give Cuttach any more honour in a world where poverty-stricken tacksmen and their families were at the receiving end of the raids, not the anti-Jacobite nobles, it does perhaps explain his initial motives.

It's a full year after the Lismore drover was beaten up outside the pub at Appin, before there's another account of the gang's raids, again with threats of violence and this time evidence of a different technique emerging, more in line with the classic highwayman's ambush of Hollywood legend. The modern road from Lochgilphead to Oban follows in part the route of the old road, and although not as much frequented as the likes of e.g. Midmuir, one could imagine that in winter it would be a more sheltered and easier route, so long as the rivers and bogs could be forded easily. It was certainly safer and cheaper since it was widely acknowledged that Cuttach and his gang extracted protection money from Midmuir travellers. As of December 1697, the lowland route wasn't safe any more. The land in the vicinity of Dunadd on this Lochgilphead road is largely open flat bog stretching out to the waters of a sea loch. Midway between Dunadd and Shirvuan, a track leads off over a bog with rocky, wooded hillocks on one side, probably owned in the 17th century by Campbell of Rhudle [17]. The farmstead of Rhudle still sits by this track and a pile of oaky crags and rocks sits beside it. Even today, anyone wishing to remain unseen by travellers on the main road would need to just bob down behind these rocks; all it would need would be a few more trees, a low mist and a thirty yard dash to bring any raiders face-to-face with foot traffic on the road.

One winter's midday, a group of four travellers, a chapman Archibald MacKillop, with John Campbell and Walter MacIlvernock (both local men from just down the road; the others probably thought they'd be safe with a couple of locals escorting them) and John Runt, a merchant from Inveraray, were on the road north of Lochgilphead just at this spot, when Cuttach himself and a reasonably inexperienced gang-member, one Kenneth O'Conochir, attacked them with drawn swords and bended guns. Naturally, they wanted money, and naturally, they got it. Ironically, the guns may not have been loaded, since the last time the Highlands were gripped by famine, affecting trade in all sorts of goods, ammunition was in extremely short supply [18]. Perhaps the drover they'd robbed the previous month had inadvertently paid for the ammunition, or perhaps the gang had done another raid which wasn't reported, stealing them as part of the haul.

Whatever the history behind this raid, one can't help wondering if the Inveraray merchant who was one of the victims, was the cause the following day, of an account of the incident in the justiciary records. Before Colin Campbell, baillie of Inveraray, acting as substitute for the Earl's brother, the gang's activities are noted as including robbery, theft, force, and plunder at the fairs and markets at Kilmore, Clachan Seil, Ford, Kilmartin and Kilmichael, taking quantities of merchant ware, goods, gear and money, extracting blackmail, singly or together, disturbing the public peace and generally terrifying travellers and the law-abiding inhabitants of Argyll by their 'capital crimes'. In their absence, the whole gang are declared outlaw and fugitive, and the classic announcement made by the horn and the three proclamations of "Oh Yes" made at the mercat cross in Inveraray [19]. The fates of Cuttach and his men were sealed.

FOOTNOTES

1. One of the glens in question is Glen Feochan in Kilmore parish; 'plump cattle' are mentioned in the Lament to MacDonnaich Glen Feochan, Oban Times 17.8.1901; the Dalnacabaig Grace, Oban Times 23.4.1934 mentions the sea's 'rich harvest'; the Second Statistical Account states that the 'valleys' are 'cultivated and fertile', and the late Kathie MacColl, formerly of Dalnacabeag talked of the vast quantities of soft fruit produced in former times.
2. Glencoe and EHW, p. 438.
3. Ibid. p. 439.
4. The author's own research in the parish of Kilmore, taken from figures offered by General Roy's map of c.1750 and her own site research on abandoned dwellings and enclosures, indicates that

only 16 out of 33 sites probably extant in c.1690 were still extant in c.1750. Discounting the shielings and outfield settlements, this figure rises to 16 out of 26.

5. Two shielings are clearly indicated on modern maps of Midmuir, indicating two original farmsteads, of which only one existed in the 18th century. The remains of the other is further towards Loch Nant (grid ref. 967 233, NM 82/92, Oban (South) and Kilninver) and at the foot of a track leading to Loch a Bharrain, on the south west shores of which there may have been a third shieling, complete with corn kiln, charted and investigated by the author in the late 1990s. No grid reference is available.

6. Just Rec, p. 161.

7. Ibid. p. 194.

8. Craigentaggart in Glen Feochan, sitting at the foot of the peat track mentioned in footnote 20, chapter 2.

9. Glencoe and EHW, p. 20.

10. Just Rec, p. 163.

11. Although the references within this paragraph are too numerous to mention individually, many of them are to be found in the records of the trials, in Just Rec, pp. 137-189, or other sources e.g. HCC or the Duke of Argyll's Chartularies or the 1688 Valuation Rolls, both of the latter of which are available at Argyll and Bute County Archives, Manse Brae, Lochgilphead. The reference to MacGregor's changing their name in line with a Privy Council ruling has a reference in Glencoe and EHW, p. 373.

12. Ibid. p. 52.

13. Ibid. pp. 152-221.

14. Ibid. pp. 292-297.

15. Ibid. p. 420.

16. The author's own research from published records contemporary with Cuttach's era e.g. The Minutes of the Synod of Argyll. The research was conducted by averaging the results of three randomly selected sets of locations, of the same number of mainland sites as the gang targetted.

17. Valuation Rolls 1688.

18. Glencoe and EHW, pp. 130, 139-141, 146-147.

19. Just Rec, p.164.

FOUR

Ten miles from Inveraray, round the head of Loch Fyne, and bordered by the high hills between Loch Lomond and Glen Fyne, the castle of Ardkinglas has been occupied by Campbells for centuries. At the end of the 17th century, it's hereditary owner, Sir Colin Campbell, was a long standing compatriot of Campbell of Argyll and such a major influence on local politics and social affairs that legends survive about him and his family. The castle as it would have been in Cuttach's day is now long gone, but at the time it had what was referred to as 'The Pit of Ardkinglas', now not currently identifiable. It may have been some sort of oubliette or bottle dungeon, either within or without the castle walls and if not an oubliette, at the very least fitted with manacles on the wall to hold the prisoners. The pit may have been later re-used as an ice-house after the castle was demolished and it successor built on a different site [1]. Whatever and wherever it was, in May 1698 it held the ring-leader of a notorious gang of stouthrieves; Cuttach Campbell was in the hands of the authorities for a third time. As before, they didn't hold him for long. With or without the help of his gang, Cuttach escaped and was soon plying his trade again across the hills of Lorn. [2]

This apparent ease with which gang members escape from their various prisons is one of the curiosities of Cuttach's gang. There are other instances in the justiciary records of prisoners escaping, especially from the notoriously insecure Inveraray castle or the tolbooth [3], but for the same man (Cuttach himself) or for the same gang to do so repeatedly may point at something more sinister going on. Conditions in prisons all over the country at that time were as bad as our modern minds can imagine. At the very worst, the inmates would be flung into a cold, occasionally flooded, unventilated chamber with no light, no sanitation and no contact with the outside world except when the gaoler arrived daily to lower mouldy bread and sour meat into the cell – if you were lucky! In rather better conditions, the cell might have a small barred window, through which the prisoner could hear the outside world or the viewing public may be permitted to parade past to glory at the prisoner's plight. In many cases, execution was a blessed alternative to a long period in custody, the latter ideally serving as precursor to punishment rather than the punishment itself.

Even allowing for the insecurity of Inveraray castle however, one has to question whether there was some other process or the involvement of some person which contributed to the gang members' repeated escapes from custody. The technique of slipping out of the castle due to the dodgy masonry can't have been used at the gaol or the Pit of Ardkinglas, and after the first one or two escapes, the prison authorities would surely be suspicious of e.g. an unusually hirsute lady visitor hiding her face and clutching a large parcel! Cuttach's gang seemed to have so many blackmail targets and so many contacts right across the county that one wonders if someone at the gaol, the castle, Ardkinglas, or maybe all three, was involved in their escape. If there was, then the authorities clearly didn't realise, let alone find who it was, or else that person would have faced the same fate as the gang members.

In addition to this prospect, another character involved with the gang's trials and captures has an interesting angle when all the information is viewed together. Colin Campbell of Ellangreig, the baillie of Inveraray, a mature man (he may even have been a grandfather by then) who must have had some considerable local connections as part of his work with the courts, was involved with bonds and business deals across Lorn [4]. Not quite the equivalent of an English bailiff, he nevertheless would have mixed with the most respectable figures in society and appeared to have his fingers in as many legal pies as he could. No question was made as to his integrity in such matters and everything was very upright and decent.

It hadn't been quite so decent and upright some years previously. At the trial of Duncan Clerk in 1691, as per normal practise, the convicted prisoners goods and properties were confiscated 'for the Crown'. On this occasion, these goods amounted to a horse and eight cattle of both genders and various ages and they'd all been cared for during Duncan's trial by one John Campbell of Dergachy. A fortnight after Duncan's execution, a team ('gang' perhaps?) of twelve men, headed by Colin Campbell of Ellangreig and his son, went to Dergachy's land and removed all the animals, to which Dergachy himself 'made no opposition'. So problematic is the issue of getting the animals returned to the court authorities, that a libelled summons of riot has to be raised against the team, and eventually Colin Campbell and a few others confess their crime, and a couple of tacksmen from the gang return all but two of the animals. No questions are asked about the missing two; one may have already been in the cooking pot, the other (a horse) perhaps untraceable, since one man was a change house tacksman and the animal may have been sent off with a guest, as part of the normal horse-swapping practise at change houses.

As a result of this unusual criminal behaviour for a respectable gentryman, Colin Campbell of Ellangreig and Campbell of Dergachy (both Dunoon peninsula men) are fined £100 each, and the others in the team or gang, £50 each.[5]

In future years, Colin Campbell appears to be trying to restore his reputation. He gains a bailliage at Inveraray just in time for Cuttach's gang to come to the fore, being on the jury at John MacColl's trial and acting judge when the gang are declared outlaw in 1697.[6]

When examined in greater detail, Campbell of Ellangreig's involvement in the whole issue of Cuttach's gang hints at something extra going on. Colin had been a loyal compatriot to the Royalist Earl of Argyll only a few years before [7], and if the theory about Cuttach's gang being Jacobite is true, then he may have seen their involvement in Duncan Clerk's criminal career as being part of the latter's downfall. Colin's home parish, Inverchaolain, embracing the shores of Loch Striven, is next door to Duncan Clerk's parish, and it's Colin himself who receives Duncan's confession – who knows what other wee requests Duncan may have made to a familiar local laird, or what reassurances Colin gave him in return. Perhaps he thought that Duncan's fate wouldn't have come about if his criminal mentor hadn't interfered in his life in the first place – and then for that Jacobite mentor to disappear into the hills when Duncan was captured would surely have raised the ire of a Royalist laird, local to Duncan's parish.

Colin couldn't have overturned the judgement of the court, and there's never any mention of wife and family for Duncan (apart from his deceased son John), but the confiscation of all the latter's goods before they were given over to the Procurator Fiscal may indicate that Colin was trying to retrieve something of worth out of the property of an executed man, and not for his own purposes. Duncan was after all, if not a vassal of Colin's, then a vassal of one of the neighbouring Campbell lairds and there's an unusual number of Clerks in the team which made off with the confiscated property.

Come the time of trial for Cuttach's men, Colin Campbell is on the jury for that of John MacColl[8]; was he more determined than his fellow jurors to see justice done to the whole gang? It seems a strange situation for a man who (despite his role as baillie), had a criminal conviction, to be allowed on the jury when a similar case is being tried. He's even in the judgement seat to proclaim Cuttach's entire criminal clan outlaws[9]; was he still fighting the cause of the long-dead Duncan Clerk?

Whether or not Campbell of Ellangreig's path was deliberately crossing that of Cuttach's, after the latter's escape from custody at Ardkinglas, he must have taken the news of the gang's outlawing back with him to their Loch na String headquarters. From now on, their activities and raid techniques appear to change. The simple, almost naive, raids on small farmsteads, coming away with the odd cow or a barrel of oats seem to be restricted to targets in the North of the county, or to tacksmen who haven't paid their protection money dues. In the Southern districts of Argyll and Lorn, other types of raiding are now being conducted – apparently motiveless ones, and certainly more involved and violent; goods, weapons, food and money are taken, and if they never took a human life it wasn't for want of trying.

The highway robberies which Cuttach's gang made on Midmuir travellers doubtless also continued, although with the prevailing famine there wouldn't be as many drovers on the road, and this perhaps contributed to the gang's depradations on farmsteads and merchant travellers instead. Midmuir itself is today a weather-beaten stretch of open bog and moor, the site of a wind farm, and with ruins of farmsteads, shielings and older dwellings scattered along its route. Along the old track and almost a mile and a quarter from the current Musdale road are a patch of crags forming a miniature ravine nearly a hundred yards long and at its narrowest only wide enough to admit two or three people abreast; certainly not wide enough for a couple of mounted riders or (in modern times) a large four-wheel-drive vehicle. Enormous service pipes are currently perched at the top of one side of the ravine, but clearly before this excavation, the slope on this side, mirroring the scrubby crag on the other, would form the only possible site along this half of the track, where waiting thieves could ambush travellers. At one point, the ravine narrows and turns in such a way that someone approaching from Midmuir farm couldn't see or be seen by someone (or some gang!) hiding behind the rocks just yards from them. One can't help wondering, with the farmstead being just visible from the top of the ravine, whether this was the spot at which Cuttach's gang did their Midmuir work.

Whether or not the gang were still blackmailing Midmuir travellers, by the beginning of 1699, they were still predating change houses where travellers would stay overnight. In the very northernmost reaches of the parish of Kilmichael the ruined change house of Glennan lies on the side road to the village of Ford with a wee bog and the earthwork remains of the dwelling known as Tighachar beside it. The change house itself appears to have been far larger than Tighachar, but the latter is listed as being the home of Patrick MacGregor and his family. They'd recently changed their name to Campbell, and one night in February while he and his family were asleep, three of Cuttach's gang (one of the MacColls with them) broke into the house. The justiciary records state that it was Tighachar they broke into, but judging by the haul the gang took, it seems more likely that it was the change house of Glennan next door; perhaps Patrick and the family slept in the wee house beside it, like with many family-run hotels today; it may have been the only way that Patrick didn't hear (or at least didn't do anything about challenging) the raiders. That night, the gang members took over £104 worth of goods (around two and half years income for a tenant farmer[10]), clearing the house of whisky, silver, food, clothing, yarn and weapons[11]. Around the same time, ten miles away over the hills at the head of Loch Tralaig, a chapman was robbed by the same gang members of what little money he had, and probably all his tobacco.[12]

The curious thing about this latter chapman raid is how close it was to the gang's headquarters on Loch na String. At the time, the path marked on old maps[13] as running to and beyond the little farmstead of Drumnashellig by Loch Tralaig may have continued up the burn leading into the hills and directly towards Loch na String. The contours of the land as it is now certainly indicate that the path may have continued in this direction even though all trace of it has been wiped out by forestry workings. Whatever the issue of a path from Drumnashellig to Loch na String, it seems highly likely, with the gang's easy proclivity for crossing vast tracts of hillside in half a night, that an ambush of a passing chapman was conducted directly from Cuttach's Loch na String headquarters. It certainly indicates that there was some sort of direct route to and from Loch Tralaig and Loch na String, which has an influence on the details of their final, fatal raid.

By this time however, new gang members appear to have been coming thick and fast, with a few old hands always accompanying them on raids. Cuttach however isn't seen on any of these later raids; perhaps he's middle-aged by now, and taking advantage of the size of the gang, and the respect he's receiving as ring-leader; perhaps his last escape from custody reinforced his unwillingness to sally forth with his men. On a sunny day when you're young and healthy, being in the hills is a wonderful experience. Any adversity of weather, age, ill health or in the case of the gang, not having eaten for days, doesn't make for a good time. The night after the raid on the Glennan change house, there was probably feasting and carousing on the island on Loch na String, while the change house master and his family probably didn't sleep well for months.

Within weeks of the Glennan raid, there was another one, equally vicious, so that gang-members operating in the south of the county seem to be characterising themselves for the violence of their raiding technique.

It all started with Hugh Cameron and two MacEans (MacDonalds) from Glencoe meeting up somewhere in Lorn. It may have been at the gang headquarters, but it may equally have been at the market at Kilmartin, since they went together to the residence of a relation of one of the Glencoe men, Duncan Roy Campbell, living in the parish. There they met with one of Duncan's servants (personally I can't help wondering just how willing the servant was), and another tacksman from the same farmstead. Together, the six men journeyed to Loch Fyneside to the house of one Archibald Campbell in Nether Kames where they stayed for a full day and night, perhaps waiting for better weather. Historians have mixed opinions as to the identity of the old 'Nether' Kames, but in the middle of the 18th century it was certainly the settlement closest to the loch waters[14], which would correspond today with East Kames. The current East and Middle Kames now sit in their own wee bay by the loch, hidden from above by trees and only really visible from the water. Whether there were trees there in 1699 is unknown, but the place would have certainly been sheltered, and Archie Campbell may have known what good pickings lay on the opposite side of the loch. It's only when one stands at the water's edge though, that one is struck with the magnitude of the task the men had. It was night-time, it was April so the weather may not have been too good, and the loch is choppy and wide at the best of times. To transport seven men over to their next target, they would probably have needed a reasonable sized sail boat, which begs the question – why didn't their neighbours notice? Perhaps they did, but were too scared to do anything about it until it was too late.

Over at the other side of Loch Fyne, a house in the farmstead of Lergy was short of five sheep come the morning. Whatever the size of sheep in 17th century Argyll, (and at a time of famine one could imagine they weren't the huge beasts of modern times), the records state that the seven gang members, once they had them back at Kames, slaughtered, dressed and ate the lot. Suitably refreshed, they gathered another couple of gang members, some weapons and presumably some ponies and set off south towards Lochgilphead. Now a busy county town, Lochgilphead at the time would have been a scatter of farmsteads around the village set into a shallow bowl of land, with the waters of a sea loch at its base. The farmstead of Fernoch, still a working business, sits on the edge of this bowl of land and at the time of the raid was the dwelling of MacLarty the miller, evidently a man of some wisdom and wiliness.

When the gang broke into the miller's house, wielding their weaponry and demanding goods, gear and money, the miller appears to have challenged them to a certain extent. Why else would they have threatened him to the fear of his life? Fortunately, he escaped, and fortunately, there's no mention of him having a family; unfortunately, the gang made off with food, the miller's sword, clothing and 'other plenishings'[15]. If they stole his sword, did he perhaps try to defend his house with it and they wrestled it from him? And against such a vicious band of stouthrieves, how on earth did he escape? Were they drunk, and was miller MacLarty just not prepared to die? Does it infact indicate, once again, that people were beginning to fight back?

All the spoils from the Lochgilphead raid were taken back to Duncan Roy Campbell's house in Kilmartin parish, where it was all disposed of 'as they thought fit'. No doubt some of it found its way back to headquarters, since soon after that, some of the gang broke into a house close by the site of one of the chapman raids earlier in the year, taking leather and other goods, and they may have been making their way 'home' at the time. They certainly didn't hang around with their haul, or take it to someone's house, but simply hid it in a crag close by[16]; perhaps it was a pre-arranged pick up point with the rest of the gang. By daylight, the gang members had returned to the vicinity of Archie Campbell's house at Kames. Clearly night-time raiding was this sub-gang's speciality, as they waited on the moor above until dark before dropping down to the lochside just south of the village. Here, John Anderson's house at Kilmory was broken into (he was evidently a fisherman) and his nets, two geese, food, clothing, plenishings and even household furniture was taken, to the value of two hundred merks [17](over £133, and around three years income for John Anderson[18]).

Weighed down by all these goods, the gang returned to Craigmaddy moor and hid the lot. This time, we learn from the justiciary records where some of the haul ended up – a certain Euan MacDougall received a night-cap, a coat and four ells (almost four metres) of plaid.

By now, the people in and around the village of Lochgilphead must have been living in fear, doubting the approach of any stranger and too frightened to investigate any night-time disturbance outdoors. Somehow, Hugh Cameron, the young man first involved with Cuttach's gang three years before and the experienced (though perhaps not experienced enough!) member who held the Lochgilphead district in terror through the spring of 1699, was captured. He stood at his trial in the fenced dock at the Inveraray tolbooth infront of Mr. John Campbell, accused of theft and robbery, receipt of theft, plundering and all the usual charges; surely he knew he had no hope of an acquittal. He was swinging on the Inveraray gallows by sunset on May day.[19]

There's no indication of how Hugh was eventually captured, but the fact that his compatriots only days later lifted a large sow from Fernoch[20], the same miller's farmstead which Hugh and the others had predated only a few weeks before, seems to tell part of the story. John MacColl was amongst the gang members who conducted that raid, and at some stage around the same time, he was also captured and held in Inveraray castle, with the charge of being involved in the Kilmory raid against him. Inveraray castle was obviously still as insecure as ever (or maybe Cuttach's men remembered the escape technique!) as John was out and plying his trade again before he could come to trial.[21]

However insecure the castle may have been, someone had stepped up their game before July that same year. John

MacColl was caught again, and with him one Archibald Campbell (perhaps the man from Kames), Duncan MacPherson and Archibald MacCallum. This time, his fellow gang members couldn't help him and he and the others faced Mr.John Campbell in court at the tolbooth, as Hugh had done a few weeks before. The list of jury members on this occasion is interesting to say the least – among the few Inveraray locals and stalwarts (merchants, the local surgeon, a gardener and a maltman) were six gentrymen, all but one with an obvious connection to Campbells. One of the jurymen was Colin Campbell, the baillie of Inveraray, probably delighted to see some of his long-term enemies in custody at last, and Alexander MacDougall, a brother of MacDougall of Knipoch, another Campbell compatriot[22]. The prisoners confessed to their crimes, and although the judge seemed to want further time to consider more evidence (refreshingly perhaps indicating that he was giving the men a fair trial), it was all over by Monday morning. The four men were hanged that afternoon, and what little property they had was confiscated for the Crown (infact for the Procurator Fiscal, as the Crown's representative).[23]

These last two trials seem to leave a dent in the gang's confidence. It may have been this, or simple retribution that drew Cuttach out of his headquarters for the first time in a few years. It does appear ironic that five months after John MacColl and the others were hanged, and when a relative of MacDougall of Knipoch had been on the jury, Cuttach and another man (a newcomer, Eun MacDougall) raided MacDougall of Knipoch land at Duninveran (now Loch Avich House) of two cows. The animals are taken straight to Good

Sollar's house (similarly we haven't heard of him for a few years either), where they're killed, dressed and eaten. Not satisfied with enacting pay-back on MacDougall of Knipoch, the hides are loaded up and taken to a farmstead (now ruined) at the other end of Glen Avich, where the laird, John MacGillies, finds himself with stolen goods in his byre the following morning[24]. If this is indeed retributive for MacDougall of Knipoch's jury service at a gang member's trial, it spells different tactics – a few years before, John MacGillies would have just lost the odd pig or a barrel of grain in retribution. Now he was the target of an attempted blame-laying and at a site where although there's the classic track winding up onto the hill above, such as at so many other gang target sites, there isn't a twin one for them to approach or escape by. Something had changed in Cuttach's gang, and it wasn't long before it would change further.

With the vicious days of Hugh Cameron's sub-gang predating the Lochgilphead area finished and Cuttach perhaps having to rethink his tactics after losing John MacColl, clearly he would have to train some gang members as his deputies. The protection racket was probably still being enacted on Midmuir, and the occasional (unreported) retributive crime or highway theft conducted, but one January day Cuttach evidently decided to give young Eun MacDougall a challenge. Along with John MacCallum, he probably set off in daylight from Loch na String in filthy weather, snowing or hailing as it does in January in Argyll and turning the hilltracks into mudslides and the loch sides into bogs. Taking a circuitous route they probably came round via Bragleen and above Scammadale farmstead to the high ground above Glen Euchar on the north-west shores of Loch Scammadale. They may well have known whose farmstead lay beneath them. Bearing the same name as the brother of MacDougall of Knipoch who'd sat on the jury at John MacColl's trial, Alexander MacDougall in Lagganmore (a Royalist of the same surname was tacking the place only fifteen years previously[25]) was well respected in the community. He'd been involved in business dealings and legal bonds with the gentry for a few years and evidently was familiar with MacDougall of Knipoch, Colin Campbell, baillie of Inveraray and Colin Campbell of Bragleen[26]. He may only have been a tacksman, but he clearly had some local influence, and he was clearly on more than nodding terms with MacDougall of Knipoch and others. With such influence, he's unlikely to have been a very young man, but judging by his later behaviour he can hardly have been in creakily-jointed middle-age either.

The farmstead of Lagganmore on Loch Scammadale shore, which lay below Cuttach's two gang members that January night in 1700 was tacked by this same Alexander MacDougall. A 'yellow' cow (actually belonging to widow Mary Ewing who lived over the hills and by all accounts one of the nimble-footed Highland breed) was housed on the farm, perhaps safely tucked up in the byre or in a field close by.

With this intended raid however, there was an irony which turned the tables of fortune for Cuttach's gang. Only two generations before, a large byre among the farm buildings at Lagganmore had been the scene of a locally condemned massacre of clanspeople by the rampaging forces of Colkitto MacDonald, ostensibly a precursor to the early Jacobites. All the women, children and elderly men in the glen, along with prisoners taken from the defeated Campbell forces after a battle at Lagganmore (said to be a hundred 'souls' in total), were locked into the byre and the place set alight. Only two people escaped (one of them, a Campbell of Bragleen, through his own courage and wiliness, the other a pregnant woman who escaped through the burning roof and outran her pursuers[27]). In 1700, though the building was under use, the stones would have still borne the scorch marks of the atrocity; it was almost two more centuries before the name Barn of Bones was coined.

In the West Highlands, clan memories are long and grudges born readily. The yellow cow which Eun and his partner-in-crime were aiming to steal may have belonged to widow Ewing, but for a Jacobite raider (no matter his ring-leader's surname) to take it from Lagganmore, was touching a raw nerve.

This time, the gang chose the wrong tacksman.

FOOTNOTES

1. The Royal Commission on the Ancient and Historical Monuments of Scotland vol. 7, Mid Argyll and Cowal, medieval and later monuments, published 1992, p.212.
2. Just Rec, p. 188.
3. Ibid. e.g. pp. 67 or 70.
4. The Clan Campbell Abstracts by Sir Duncan Campbell of Barcaldine and Glenure. Available on www.archive.org?stream/clancampbellabst01camp_djvu.txt e.g. 1.8.1699 and other dates.

5. Just Rec, p. 139.
6. Ibid. p. 161.
7. HCC, p. 55.
8. Just Rec, p. 183.
9. Ibid. p. 164.
10. www.johnhearfield.com/History/Breadt/htm
11. Just Rec, p. 184.
12. Ibid. p. 185.
13. 1st edition Ordnance Survey map 1843-1882, 6" to a mile.
14. Military Survey of Scotland 1747-1755 by General Roy.
15. Just Rec, p. 172.
16. Ibid. p. 173.
17. Ibid. p. 185.
18. www.johnhearfield.com/History/Breadt/htm
19. Just Rec, p. 174.
20. Ibid. p. 185.
21. Ibid. p. 185.
22. MacDougall of Knipoch was included in a list of gentlemen heritors who signed an oath of allegiance to George I in 1715, proving himself to be a Royalist alongside Campbell of Argyll. HCC, p. 107.
23. Just Rec, p. 186.
24. Ibid. p. 187.
25. "The Commons of Argyll" by Duncan C.MacTavish, compiled c.1933-35, Lochgilphead. Available on www.clanmactavish.org
26. The Clan Campbell Abstracts by Sir Duncan Campbell of Barcaldine and Glenure. Available on www.archive.org?stream/clancampbellabst01camp_djvu.txt e.g. 1.8.1699.
27. "Records of Argyll" by Lord Archibald Campbell, published by Blackwood and Sons, Edinburgh, 1885, p. 199.

FIVE

One quiet cloudy night in December 1699, the gentlemen and heritors of Mid Lorn and Muckairn, some of whom must have travelled miles, gathered in the vicinity of Moleigh farmstead, south of what is now Oban. With Moleigh being accessible in at least two different directions (one of them closer to the road to Muckairn) it's tempting to think that they were going to try for a pincer movement on their target. This target was the house of a man surnamed MacCoul, and hidden there was John MacConochy, alias MacDougall, with a furlat (eight gallons) of corn stolen from a farm in a neighbouring glen.

For the past five months, John MacConochy had been thieving farmsteads and farmland in the immediate vicinity of the parish of which Oban is now a part. He isn't mentioned as being part of Cuttach Campbell's gang, but Cuttach must surely have heard of him (John ends up on Cuttach's own stamping ground after one theft), and perhaps the man was hoping to join the gang one day.

John MacConochy's first recorded raid is at Kilvarie, on the old road between Kilmore and Connel, and his haul on that occasion came to the value of around £40 and was later found in his possession. Since he wasn't brought into custody at that point, it may have been just a neighbour or two who came across him – they probably regretted not apprehending him afterwards!

Come December, John takes (on separate raids) a mare and a filly from Glenshellach (these finish up in Glenorchy), two gallons of corn from Soroba and three goats from Cabrachan, which he took to the lands of Bragleen and ate there.[1]

After his last raid, the one where John settled down at Moleigh for the night, the gentlemen and heritors who had gathered to apprehend him sent him to Inveraray for custody. Among these gentlemen and heritors may have been one MacDougall of Knipoch. He was certainly a heritor of Mid Lorn[2] and his home was only a couple of miles from Moleigh. Even closer was Campbell of Glenfeochan or Stronchormaig, and the laird at Dunach. Others further afield may have included Campbell of Scammadale, Campbell of Melfort, Campbell of Airds or the MacDougall lairds at Rarey and Ardincaple. Clearly a force of some considerable weight, the work of which was bound to be talked about at any local gathering for months to come. Almost certainly, the capture of John MacConochy would have been discussed in the inn at the Kilmore market, or between kirk laity at Kilninver, and almost certainly one Alexander MacDougall, the high-ranking, successful businessman who tenanted Lagganmore farmstead on Loch Scammadale shore, would have heard the tale of the gentlemen arrest-mobbers, shortly before two representatives of Cuttach Campbell's gang came sniffing around Lagganmore that January day in 1700.

As to the exact date of this January raid which Cuttach's men undertook, as with much of the gang's activities, the justiciary records don't stipulate the date except to say that it was a Sabbath. The gang weren't known for doing raids at full moons, so it seems likely it wouldn't have been the last Sunday in the month when the moon was at its largest[3]. Amongst the other Sundays, the first one on the 7th January has a quality about it which may have tempted Cuttach to make a fatal mistake. At the time that the gang was operating (before the change from Julian to Gregorian calendar), many parts of rural Britain either still observed Old Christmas Day, or the date was still very sharp in the minds of the communities. The gentry and tacksmen would of course be aware of any specific date by the use of occasional almanacs, or the task of upkeeping rent books, and the working class people would probably hear of it via announcements in kirk, or inevitably the women in the household who were always more finely attuned to dates and anniversaries. Old Christmas Day fell on the 5th or 6th January, and the ordinary people of Argyll, if they were aware of Old Christmas Day, would have celebrated it on that Saturday in 1700.

For a group of renegades such as Cuttach's gang, with no access to kirk services or meetings, rent books, almanacs or the memory-skills of womankind, it would be only too easy to mix up the odd day or two, thinking perhaps that Old Christmas Day fell on the Sunday.

There's a very old superstition about any type of Christmas Day among thieves – if they manage to steal something on Christmas Day, they'll be successful in their nefarious ventures all throughout the rest of the year.[4]

With Old Christmas Day being so close to the date of the gang's final raid, and the old superstition about thieving on Christmas Day being so prevalent, it's very tempting to think that someone in the gang thought they'd try and secure a full year's thieving by means of a raid on the 7th or (as they may have thought it was) the 6th January.

For Eun MacDougall and John MacCallum, waiting on the crags above Lagganmore farmhouse for an opportune time to strike, the day and date may have been of little import. If, as seems likely, they knew who the tacksman was, they may have realised it was wise to avoid encountering him, so waited until he and his family were out of the way. Being a Sunday, and the nearest kirks at Kilninver and Kilmelfort being then without an incumbent[5], meaning that the tacksman and his family would probably be at home, maybe the gang members waited until all the cows had been milked and the farm was quiet before making their strike. However, knowing that they would have a long day's walk over the hills ahead of them, they probably did their work as early in the morning as possible, which could have been their second mistake.

In view of a probable time of the strike being early morning, and in view of how rural working people are always busiest first and last thing in the day, it was inevitable that someone would have noticed Eun and John making off with the cow. With the gang's previous raid being at Duninveran just over the hills and Cuttach himself on that occasion accompanying Eun only days before, someone may even have recognised the gang members on this occasion.[6]

Whatever the circumstances, it seems that the tacksman in Lagganmore, and probably a farmhand or two, set off in pursuit of Eun and John and the stolen cow. Quite which direction they took is a reasonably simple matter to deduce. The modern road which Lagganmore is close to joins the main road a few hundred yards away; this current modern road still follows roughly the course of the old one through Glen Gallain heading for Kilmelfort, but in 1700 would have been far too obvious a route to take, open to view by any manner of travellers who happened to pass by. Another possible route may have been along the loch-shore up to Bragleen and into the hills via the usual track onto Loch na String. This latter route however wouldn't sit with the gang's usual method of escape (fleeing onto a track roughly opposite the target farmstead) and would also lay Eun and John open to ambush from other inhabitants, trapped between the loch-shore and the road (that's assuming that the loch wasn't in a January flood and spilling over the road). Crucially, on old maps a third route is shown[7] which, barring a crossing of the river, would be far easier for Eun and John and most importantly of all, fits with the gang's normal escape routes. Around two hundred yards from Lagganmore, this old route crosses the river, leads up onto open hill land, then runs alongside the edge of scrubby woodland and between the classic raiders' terrain of gentle crags, before meeting a forestry fence. Beyond the fence, and into the forestry trees, the route is almost obliterated, visible only as patches of rather more open and hollowed gaps between the tree trunks, as it snakes around the hill. Before the trees were planted however, a slight dip in the land as the track rounded the hill[8] would seem to have hidden it, and any thieves using it, from view of travellers on the main road below.

By the time Eun MacDougall and John MacCallum were driving widow Ewing's cow around the shoulder of the hill above Glen Gallain, Alex MacDougall from

Lagganmore may well have been close on their trail. Another gentlemen arrest-mob a few years after this time, traced their quarry by following the hoof-prints in the mud[9] (presumably at a time of year when hoof-prints wouldn't normally be following that particular track), so it's probable that Alex and his farmhand did the same; certainly, they could only have been an hour or so behind Eun and John.

The hill track which the men may have been following now peters out, still on forestry land, near the ruins of Laggananairgid farmstead on the hill above Glen Gallain. Various smaller tracks appear to criss-cross the land in the vicinity of these ruins, again probably disguised from the people there by the various slopes and humps of the hill, so it may be that Eun and John followed a now lost track towards the crags above Corrielorn, the farmstead at the edge of an open vale at the mouth of Loch Tralaig. One track in the hills above Corrielorn runs surprisingly close to Laggananairgid, disguised by the depth of the burnsides, and for the gang members, they were on reasonably familiar territory by now, having ranged the braes in this vicinity before on raids.[10]

For Alex MacDougall and his farmhand, one can't help wondering at this stage, if they really knew what they were up against? Even if one of them had recognised Eun from the Duninveran raid, they can't have known that they were heading straight for Cuttach and the remainder of the gang. If they did have some idea of the task ahead of them, did they recruit help from Laggananairgid along the way?

It's only when one stands on the side of a rain-lashed Argyll hill close to the site of one of the raiders' targets, that one sees how vast and forbidding this countryside can be at times. If Cuttach and his gang hadn't been so thoroughly callous and violent to their own people, one could have admired the hardiness of them, surviving so long in such exacting terrain. As it is, one admires more than anything, those men from Lagganmore who set out from their home early on a January morning to follow the gang members.

With such a challenging prospect before them, what kind of man was it that went after Eun and John and widow Ewing's stolen cow? At the very least, Alex MacDougall must have had some experience with a firearm – who would otherwise want to chase thieves who've proved themselves willing to use them against their victims, let alone against pursuers? The vast tracts of land Alex was covering doesn't seem to have been any problem to him either, since he appears to have kept pace with Eun and John all the way if he was able to follow their tracks in the mud or snow before those same tracks got rained on or snowed under. Certainly to follow the gang members such a distance he must have had either a degree of determination or courage or both, perhaps even a sense of responsibility to a widow who'd entrusted him with her cow, only to have it stolen. The obvious solution arises when considering Alex MacDougall's behaviour, faced with two stouthrieves making off with property that wasn't even his own: could he have had military or semi-military experience, perhaps learnt during some time with the Watch-keepers? As a tacksman, he wouldn't have held a commission in the Watch, but men of such social classes were culled from the laird's tenantry to hold ranks surely equal to those of the professional soldiery: sergeants, corporals etc, all undoubtedly handpicked by the commissioned gentry. With all the evidence to hand, and viewing the way that Alex MacDougall readily took to the hills in pursuit when the cow was taken, it wouldn't be surprising if the tacksman in Lagganmore had served his time on the Nether Lorn Watch.

Once above the farmstead of Corrielorn, both Eun and John with the cow, and Alex MacDougall with whatever reinforcements he'd been able to summon up along the way, would see a broad sweep of land ahead of them, unless the mist and rain were shrouding it. Settled into the land with the modern road at one end and the remains of old farmtowns at the other, Loch Tralaig, on the flood plains of which Corrielorn sits, is a boggy-edged, midge-swarming stretch of inland water typical of Nether Lorn. Old tracks skirt the flood plain, hugging the side of the hill, and the gang members had certainly trod this terrain before. At the head of the loch, close to where a couple of Eun's comrades had ambushed the travelling merchant for his tobacco and his money eleven months previously, the farmtown of Druimnashellig sat at the foot of a track leading up into the hills. This same track may have led directly to Loch na String, and if Alex and his assistants knew who the men they were following were, their hearts must have been in their mouths at this point. As it was, with nightfall quickly coming on, and if Eun and John were indeed following hill tracks all the way from Lagganmore, they wouldn't have far to go by now.

In addition to the track leading from Druimnashellig, another twisted onto the slopes of the hill from its neighbouring farmtown, Polanduich, further round the head of the loch. Even today, this latter route almost reaches the summit of the highest point of land locally[11] (Cruach Narrachan) although currently incorporated into forestry tracks. If the men and their pursuers were following this path, and dependant on the weather and the stamina of Eun and John, and Alex and his assistants, they may have decided to hole up somewhere for the night around here. Between Lagganmore and the gang's eventual destination is only a distance of eight miles, and the old-time drovers covered around ten or twelve in a day[12]. The drovers however didn't do their work in the middle of winter with severely limited daylight hours, and if Eun had realised Alex was on his tail, he may have been putting in more miles, twisting and turning to try to shake him off. Certainly if, as seems likely, Alex kept pace with Eun all the way, they'd both have been forced to set up camp for the night at around the same time (in the vicinity of Polanduich or Druimnashellig), each probably wondering if the other would still be there come the morning.

Fortunately, or unfortunately, for both of them, they were still there first thing on Monday morning. Although Alex wouldn't know it at the time, Eun's destination was only the other side of the hill at this point. The tracks leading down the southern shoulders of Cruach Narrachan are now covered by the forestry trees, but the contours of the land as depicted on the modern maps, hint at some sort of possible access via the burns and the gentler slopes almost to the shores of Loch Avich where the gang had done so much work recently.

Settled now into the claustrophobic surrounds of the trees, the ruins of the old Kilmun house on Loch Avich shore, close by the mouth of the track leading to Loch na String, depict what was obviously once an impressive two-storey house with added wings, and a large yard or garden at the front. Clearly an influential dwelling in its time, it is however doubtful that it's the one which stood on the spot in 1700, although the remains of the outbuildings could be older. Exactly where its outbuildings were can only be guessed, but at this date, at least one of the buildings on the site and described as a 'house' rather than a byre, was unused, probably due to the effects of the recent famine. The tacksman in Kilmun had died only seven years before and although he had brothers, these men may have had their own tack and been unable to take it up[13]. History doesn't record who, if anyone, was tacking Kilmun at the time, but it, along with the neighbouring land encompassing Narrachan and Duninveran was all MacDougall of Knipoch owned, the same gentryman whose brother had been a juror at John MacColl's trial the previous year. It's not stated where widow Ewing was living at the time, although there are men of the same surname as her late husband living at Narrachan eight years before.[14]

Waiting in the peat loft of this empty property at Kilmun that Monday morning in January 1700, Lachlan Cuttach Campbell and his fellows may have seen Eun and John driving widow Ewing's cow down the slopes of the hill. Almost certainly, they didn't see Alex and his assistants. At some point around this time, however, the tacksman from Lagganmore must have realised the enormity of the task before him and just how many more assistants and weapons he would need. With the entire gang gathered in the empty building by the loch-shore (and ultimately feasting on the widow's cow) there was no way that the few farmhands and tacksmen he'd have been able to recruit as he went along could have apprehended them all. If at no other stage in the chase, the behaviour of Alex MacDougall now surely betrays some sort of semi-military training. He could have easily risked his own life and the lives of his farmhands by attempting to take Cuttach's gang with only a handful of men, invariably losing most of the gang back into the hills. The justiciary records clearly state however, that Cuttach's men were in the house for two full nights before Alex pounced[15]. With a sizeable and vicious band of men to apprehend, it seems completely feasible that Alex sent for reinforcements and wisely spent those two nights and a day watching and waiting for them to arrive.

The reinforcements clearly did arrive and one can imagine they included a gentryman or two, some more strapping farmhands or merchants from along the road at Kilmelford or Dalavich, perhaps someone from Duninveran who would know the inside of the house well, and plenty of precious guns, whether loaded or not. At what time of day the house at Kilmun was stormed is impossible to judge, but once subdued (and Cuttach's gang probably fought tooth and nail!), the question arises as to how they transported them into custody. Undoubtedly, each gang member would have been tied up at wrist and ankle (or else there would be a risk of them making a run for it at the first opportunity) and a cart or carts of some sort therefore procured to carry them. There must have been around nine or a dozen men to keep hold of, and at some stage en route to Inveraray they'd have to spend the night in secure accommodation, perhaps the cellars of some local gentryman, or in the local kirk. It's a sad testimony to the loss of local tradition and history that no stories currently exist about what must have been quite an important event, as Cuttach's gang passed through the countryside on the way to their final destination.

The shortest route available for Alex MacDougall and his assistants to transport the prisoners to Inveraray was over 22 miles long and involved a short ferry journey; any other way would have meant adding considerably more miles onto the journey and further overnight stays, all of which increased the risk of the prisoners escaping. In addition, if they did take this shortest route (down to Loch Awe shore and along to Kilchrenan, then over the loch to Sonachan before picking up the southbound road to Inveraray at Cladich), they would be able to hand over responsibility for the prisoners to the high-ranking gentryman with a Watch officer in his family, whom Campbell of Sonachan was. If Kilmun was stormed early in the morning, then the convenient resting place of Kilchrenan kirk would be available to hold the prisoners overnight; in that case, perhaps someone went ahead over the loch to warn Campbell of Sonachan that his services would be needed first thing the following day.

Whichever route Alex and the men took in order to bring their prisoners into custody, once at Inveraray, and held in the castle (someone must have made the place more secure recently), with the days passing and no remaining compatriots available to help them escape, one can imagine the arguments, the blame-laying and the desperation that went through the gang. Young Eun MacDougall was the first to confess his crimes[16]. Although certainly not as experienced as many of the other gang members, it seems he was cocky enough to lead the Lagganmore raid, and with the noose already hanging over his head, one wonders why he confessed before the others. Did the authorities, knowing that he was inexperienced, think it would be easier to force a confession out of him, therefore convicting all the gang in one fell swoop? Or did Eun think he would come in for better treatment while in custody if he confessed early?

Whatever his or the authorities reasoning, Eun stood in the dock before the justiciar, MP John Campbell of Mamore (the Duke's brother and a nobleman with a young family of his own). In the days of King James, Campbell of Mamore had had the death penalty on his own head, but had managed to have it reduced to banishment, until the political tables turned and the Jacobites were ousted[17]. If Cuttach's gang were indeed early Jacobites, and the authorities knew about it, it must surely have coloured the thinking of the staunch royalist sitting in the judgement seat that day.

Standing before John Campbell, young Eun MacDougall confessed to stealing widow Ewing's cow (along with John MacCallum), and another two animals with Cuttach, along with receiving stolen goods. This latter crime would appear to have been the occasion when a Eun MacDougall received a few of the pieces taken from John Anderson's house in Kilmory by some of Hugh Cameron's sub-gang the previous April.

At this stage in the trial of the gang, two months after their capture and arrest on the shores of Loch Avich, several 'famous' witnesses were summoned for 'furder verification' of their capital crimes. One can't imagine Alex MacDougall in Lagganmore not being called up, and probably a few gentrymen whose lands were predated. Widow Ewing probably stayed at home; unless a woman was a primary witness, they don't seem to have been summoned to the court, which for later historians is disappointing since there's no better a person to recount the finer details of a story than an auld Highland wifie!

Eventually, on Thursday 14th March, before John Campbell of Mamore and Procurator Fiscal William Inglis, the entire gang were charged with 'theft, receipt of theft, stouthrief, robbery, oppression, exacting of blackmail, and breaking of prisons'. Described as being 'heinous and atrocious...ane compact of villany and wickedness... constantly there several years bygone especially the said Lauchlane as the ringleader and nurserer of many other villains' [18]. It's readily acknowledged that further crimes have been reported, but that it's pointless noting them all.

Clearly at some stage Cuttach himself was questioned and the true character of the man shows through here. When asked about the various raids the gang had done and faced with the ultimate punishment, whether or not he confessed to them all, he tried to wheedle out of responsibility for one raid, blaming the cause of it on his long-term friend and valuable gang member, Good Sollar MacIntyre. It was a debt he owed Good Sollar, he said. There was apparently no loyalty in Cuttach for his comrades in crime, and he even tried to excuse himself of the theft of another animal, saying it was a repayment of a debt from someone at Ederlines. This latter debt was probably the protection money the Ederlines tacksman hadn't paid him!

With the witnesses testimonies and the prisoners' confessions heard, the waiting jury retired to the kirk next door. The jury thus assembled had been drawn from the great and good of the Inveraray district, including amongst them a 97 year old former provost[19] and his son John Brown, a provost himself by the time he dies; one of the locally influential Duncanson family; a merchant; the baillie Colin Campbell of Ellangreig; another baillie; the laird from one of the gang's raiding targets; the local surgeon; a gardener; a couple of extra Campbells, including a gentryman; and four other men, one of them a MacDougall and another a tacksman. With most of them having served on a jury before, all the gentrymen knowing each other socially and Colin Campbell of Ellangreig perhaps having a preconceived notion of the accused's guilt, the discussions that took place would have been interesting to hear. The working class jurors, or the tacksmen, would be deferential to their landlords, but in any group of people of course there's always one who rebels, and despite the confessions of the gang, it would be interesting to speculate whether there was any challenge to the expected verdict. As it turned out, the jury emerged from the confines of the kirk with a unanimous decision which John Brown, their spokesman, would have handed to the dempster, Duncan MacIlvory. Before all the court, prisoners included, the sealed paper would have been opened and the expected 'doom' pronounced for Cuttach and his gang.

This wasn't however the end of the day's activities for the court. At the same time, the man or men who were captured by the gentlemen of Mid Lorn and Muckairn at Moleigh a few weeks before Cuttach had been apprehended, were also put in the dock, and also subject to the due process of law. The same verdict was returned on them.[20]

As outlaws, it's doubtful whether there would be coffins or even 'winding cloths' waiting in the carts for Cuttach and his gang as they emerged from custody for the last time[21]. There would certainly have been more than one cart for the number of men being shuggled the short journey down to the foreshore, and with the infamy of the gang, the ordinary inhabitants of Inveraray would surely have turned out to see justice done. It must have been a rare sight to see so many criminals 'turned off' in one go; there must have been a valuable bit of extra income for the rope maker in Inveraray that day, and this may have contributed to the wait of forty-eight hours before the time of execution.[22]

In addition to Cuttach, Eun and the newcomer who went with Eun on the final raid, there would have been the two or more prisoners apprehended at Moleigh, along with Good Sollar and the remaining MacColl from Appin, John MacAlister, Kenneth O'Chonochir, John MacLauchlane, Donald MacNokaird, John Campbell, Dugald Campbell and (less likely) the various men who worked with Hugh Cameron in 1699, and who weren't with him when he was caught. No-one will ever know if any of the gang had escaped before being apprehended; if anyone was left in the hills, or at Loch na String, there's no mention of them, although another, smaller but more wide-ranging, gang were captured just a few years later on Leckan Moor, using the same gentlemen-mob technique. Unlike other captures, there's no mention at their trial of specifically being associated with Cuttach's gang.

It's not easy now to trace the site of the original gallows, close to what was once the Old Town of Inveraray. Time, weather, water and successive Duke's landscaping have done such a good job that much above ground evidence of even the finer structures of the Old Town are almost lost. The gallows, judged by one source to have been sited on what is now a tree-topped mound by the main road, possibly by another under the site of the New Town, has certainly disappeared[23]. Wherever it was, it lay within sight of Kilmaluaig burial ground, just to the north of the present town, and with ironically beautiful views, even in bad weather, across the loch.

There is a common misconception that the old-days highwayman was the romantic buccaneer of Hollywood films. The truth is far more brutal. Violent muggings, house breakings, threats with guns and swords and almost a reign of terror came from a group of renegades in Argyll who although they never took a human life, it wasn't for want of trying. Cuttach Campbell and his remaining fellows met their end at Inveraray between the hours of 2 and 3 pm on Saturday 16th March 1700. History doesn't relate and it's perhaps needless to speculate, where their remains were interred. Suffice it to hope that their like, and the like of their compatriots, never tread the hills of Argyll ever again.

FOOTNOTES

1. Just Rec, p. 190.
2. HCC, p. 107.
3. www.eclipse.gsfc.nasa.gov/phase/phases1601.html
4. Specifically 'Lordings All Of You I Warn', a carol from

the Harleian manuscript at the British Museum, or "The Encyclopaedia of Superstitions, Folklore and the Occult" edited by Cora Linn Daniels and S. M. Stevans, published by Minerva Group 2003, reprint from 1903, p. 1500; more generally it seems to be a widespread, ancient tradition that whatever one is doing on Christmas or New Year's Day, one will be doing (successfully) the remainder of the year, c. f. "The Oxford Dictionary of Superstitions" edited by Iona Opie and Moira Tatem, published by Oxford University Press 2005, pp. 188, 261, 283 etc.

5. Fasti Ecclesiae Scoticanae volume 4, Argyll, Perth and Stirling, by Hew Scott, published by Oliver and Boyd, Edinburgh, 1973, p. 96.
6. Just Rec, p. 187.
7. Ordnance Survey map 1843-1882, 1st edition six inch.
8. OS Pathfinder map 355 (NM81/91) Kilmelford.
9. Just Rec, p. 194.
10. Just Rec, e.g. p. 185.
11. According to the RCAHMS website, the track travels approximately east from Polanduich and skirts Bar na Choil to the north-east and east, then dips round to the south, picking up a twisting track travelling approximately east-north-east to Cruach Narrachan.
12. Drove Roads, pp. 35-38.
13. From the private research done by Tony Dalton, Maolochy, Kilmelford. Commisariot Records of Argyll, Inventories, p. 18, parish of Kilchrenan.
14. Ibid. The Fencible Men of Argyll, Knipoch land, Narrachan, John MacDougall.
15. Just Rec, pp. 187-188.
16. Ibid. p. 188.
17. HCC, p. 289.
18. Just Rec, p. 187ff.
19. The Royal Commission on the Ancient and Historical Monuments of Scotland volume 7, Mid Argyll and Cowal, medieval and later monuments, published 1992, p. 117, item 65.
20. Just Rec, p. 91.
21. It was customary for outlaws to be denied any normal process of

law, hence the term 'out law', i.e. outside the law, so their bodies may have been treated with similar disdain.
22. Just Rec, pp. 186 and 189.
23. Local tradition in Inveraray, including the staff at Inveraray Jail Museum, indicate that the 'burial mound' on the 19th century Ordnance Survey maps which lay between Ivy Cottage and Kilmalieu burial ground just off the main road north-east of the current town, was the site of the gallows. Documentary references to this can be traced to the Second Statistical Account of 1845 when it is stated that bones were once found here and P. MacIntyre's "Inveraray, it's scenery and associations" (1909). Certainly the RCAHMS state that there appears to be an underlying structure and that an early Christian ring was once found at the foot of the mound. The spot is still visible on Google Earth, surrounded by an octagonal fence, and p. 28 of "Inveraray and the Dukes of Argyll" by Ian G. Lindsay and Mary Cosh, published Edinburgh University Press, 1973, has a map (c.1722) which shows 'Gallows Green' on the North shore of the River Aray where it joins the loch. However, there is also a similar 'Gallows Foreland Point' on the loch shore, approximately under the site of the New Town, and ironically close to the Inveraray Jail Museum.

ABBREVIATIONS IN FOOTNOTES

HCC - "A History of Clan Campbell" volume 3 by Alastair Campbell of Airds, published by Edinburgh University Press Ltd 2004.

Glencoe and EHW - "Glencoe & the End of the Highland War" by Paul Hopkins, published by John Donald, Edinburgh, 1986.

Drove Roads - "The Drove Roads of Scotland" by A.R.B. Haldane, published by Thomas Nelson and Sons Ltd 1952.

Just Rec – "The Argyll Justiciary Records, 1664 – 1705" published by the Stair Society 1949.

SELECT BIBLIOGRAPHY

"Minutes of the Synod of Argyll volume 2, 1652-1661" published by the Stair Society 1944.

The Royal Commission on the Ancient and Historical Monuments of Scotland, Argyll volume 2, Lorn, 1974.

"Military Survey of Scotland 1747-55" by General Roy; online version via the National Library of Scotland website.

maps.nls.uk/Scotland/index.html (The National Library of Scotland Map Library website).

1st edition OS map 1843-82, 6" to a mile.

"Inveraray and the Dukes of Argyll" by Ian G. Lindsay and Mary Cosh, published Edinburgh University Press, 1973.